WINNING NEW BUSINESS

WINNING NEW BUSINESS

Essential selling skills for non-sales people

Richard Denny

KOGAN PAGE

London and Philadelphia

Publisher's note

Every possible effort has been made to ensure that the information contained in this book is accurate at the time of going to press, and the publishers and author cannot accept responsibility for any errors or omissions, however caused. No responsibility for loss or damage occasioned to any person acting, or refraining from action, as a result of the material in this publication can be accepted by the editor, the publisher or the author.

First published in Great Britain and the United States in 2007 by Kogan Page Limited

120 Pentonville Road   525 South 4th Street, #241
London N1 9JN   Philadelphia PA 19147
United Kingdom   USA
www.kogan-page.co.uk

ISBN 978 0 7494 5009 0

British Library Cataloguing-in-Publication Data

A CIP record for this book is available from the British Library.

Library of Congress Cataloging-in-Publication Data

Denny, Richard, 1944-
  Winning new business: essential selling skills for non-sales people / Richard Denny
      p. cm.
  Includes bibliographic references
  ISBN 978-0-7494-5009-0
  1. Selling 2. Sales management 3. Marketing I. title
  HF5438.25.D46 2007
  658.85--dc22

                                                                    2007030123

Typeset by Jean Cussons Typesetting, Diss, Norfolk
Printed and bound in Great Britain by MPG Books Ltd, Bodmin, Cornwall

Dedication

This book is for my wife Dorothy whose love has been my strength and purpose, and has given my life direction.

Contents

About the Author

Richard Denny is the most inspirational business speaker in the United Kingdom. He is probably unique in that his presentations not only motivate, inspire and educate his audiences, they take away and are able to use highly practical ideas that achieve enhanced performance. He is so confident that he guarantees to get an outstanding result. If not, his fee is refundable. You can't expect better than that (and it has never happened to date).

He has sold and marketed in the Middle East, where his products included steel, cement, Yugoslavian lamb and electronic equipment. With all this vast experience he was continually being asked to speak and advise others, and this led to the Richard Denny Group being formed.

Over the past 20 years Richard has become a legend on the international speaking circuit. The Richard Denny Group is recognized as being at the forefront of business training on selling, leadership and management, customer care and business growth.

Richard has authored and presented over 30 training videos. He is the author and presenter of three audio albums. His five books – *Selling to Win, Succeed for Yourself, Motivate to Win, Speak for Yourself, Communicate to Win* – are international best-sellers, selling into 46 countries and translated into 26 languages. *Selling to Win* has become required reading for anybody who wishes to aspire to becoming a sales professional, and this book is probably the world's best seller on this subject.

Richard is the creator and founder of the British Professional Sales Diploma and the British Leadership & Management Diploma. He is also chairman of a telecommunications company in the United Kingdom.

He is a broadcaster, writer, married with four sons, and is an enthusiastic player of numerous sports. His presentations are liberally illustrated with anecdotes, people stories and of course that delightful Denny humour. Richard has the uncanny ability to delight any audience, probably because he talks common sense and has the knack of being a brilliant communicator. Apart from his experience as a keynote speaker, he also acts as a conference chairman and facilitator.

The Richard Denny Group
Cotswold Business Village
Moreton-in-Marsh
Gloucestershire GL56 0JQ
Tel: +44 (0) 1608 812424 Fax: +44 (0) 1608 651638
Email: success@denny.co.uk
Website: www.denny.co.uk

Acknowledgements

Grateful acknowledgment is made to Sony/ATV Music Publishing for permission to quote from the lyrics of Joe South's 'Walk a mile in my shoes' on page 28.

'Failure isn't fatal' by Freddie Mitman, quoted on page 141, first appeared in *On the Road to Success* (Minerva Press, 2001), and is reproduced by kind permission of the author.

I wish to thank Dorothy Denny for not only her typing skills but also and more importantly for her comments, suggestions and creativity, which made this book a joy to write.

Introduction

Let me tell you a story. In 1988 I was asked to write a book on selling, having been very fortunate in my business career and having spoken around the world on the subject for a number of years. I certainly was not a writer but I relished the challenge. I had a library with in excess of 300 business books, most of which I had not read as I found them too much like hard work. I'd been told that the only people who make money from business books are those who print them and those who publish them. I found this rather distressing as I had personally found great inspiration from the few books that I had read. However, I have to confess I found reading the majority of my library real drudgery. So I decided to write a book that would be easy to read, but more importantly would help the reader to be an outstanding success and to make money in the profession of selling.

So *Selling to Win* was written. It is now in its third updated edition, with the latest techniques for closing sales. It has been translated into 26 languages, with numerous reprints. Apparently it has become a must read for aspiring sales people. I am very honoured that my email and postbag receive daily marvellous stories from readers who have increased their sales success and their income as a result of reading that book. *Selling to Win* led to a further four books, *Motivate to Win*,

Speak for Yourself, Succeed for Yourself and *Communicate to Win*, all of which have helped their readers to achieve great success.

My publisher Kogan Page requested that I write another book on sales. I suggested the title *The Super Seller*, and started writing. I very quickly discovered that I could not add to or improve on the advice given in *Selling to Win*. As I struggled with the situation (we don't call it a problem), the deadline for completion loomed closer. I had now spent the advance, and in final desperation took a dose of my own medicine. So I took the dilemma to bed with a pad of paper. Just before going to sleep I asked my brain to find a solution. Within a few hours I awoke with the answer, and immediately wrote it down. In the morning the way forward was so obvious.

Over the past five or six years I have been speaking to numerous professional organizations and business people about winning business: from bank managers to lawyers, from accountants to architects, from vets to surveyors, and of course literally thousands of business owners. All of these people had a secondary responsibility for winning business and yet a natural dislike of selling. So this book really is for the millions of people who are an integral part of every business, but who also have to take responsibility from time to time for winning new clients, new customers, new business and most importantly of all, retaining those relationships and achieving repeat business. This book is for, and will work for, you.

What's at Stake?

There are two major causes of business failure that result in closure or bankruptcy. The first is a business's inability to sell its products or services, and the second is a business's inability to get paid on time, which leads to it running out of money. I am not going to deal with the second cause in this book. If you are a business owner there are many ways of getting your invoices paid, and if you want some help or advice on this, please contact my office. So let's concentrate on the first cause, and make sure your business does not suffer because of an inability, or even more critically an unwillingness, to sell your products or services.

Let me give you a rock of foundation. Nothing happens anywhere in the world until a sale takes place and the sales person brings in the money that everybody can eventually live off. I am sure you didn't pick up this book with a desire to become a sales person, even though in your heart of hearts you know that selling is so important. Unfortunately, the activity of selling and the label 'sales person' carries with it a stigma as well as a fear.

I have trained countless thousands of sales people in my lifetime. At the sales conferences I attend I often ask the question, 'If your careers advisor had asked you what you wanted to be when you left school, would you have replied, "I want to be a sales person"?' On only three occasions did someone raise their hand. So it seems that the majority of sales people get into that career by accident, and not necessarily as a first choice.

We have all been confronted at some stage in our lives with an untrained seller practising out-of-date sales techniques, attempting to sell us something we neither want nor need. Most of us have naturally become hardened to these outmoded tactics. We have experienced with continued frustration the unsolicited telephone calls and the rather pathetic sales gimmicks from the double glazing and home sales industry. Nevertheless, as I have already stated, selling can and should be a profession, although perhaps not equal in status to the great professions in which people take up to seven years to qualify. Many excellent professional sales people are often loath to admit that they are sales people, so they conjure up exotic titles like consultant, executive, business development manager, relationship manager and customer coordinator.

This book is not intended for the professionally employed sales person, but for the individual who from time to time has the secondary responsibility of winning new clients and customers. I shall, however, be including some highly acceptable, honest and ethical practices that will enable you to win new business.

The law of attrition states that however successful your product or service, you will lose some of your customers every year. This is of course, quite obvious: people die, they move away, their circumstances change or perhaps they take their business to a competitor. So any business that is not taking serious steps to win new business, and this of course means new customers, will sooner or later go out of business. I do realize that you may call your customers clients, so please allow me the licence to do so, but I shall never refer to them as punters.

Please let me share my passion with you, which I hope will become your passion. If you own a business or lead a department, you have the opportunity to develop a winning culture. Everyone in an organization should in some way be part of, and make some contribution towards, customer retention and winning new customers. This must be a totally shared responsibility. Of course the most valuable employee in any organization is the man or woman who can bring in the business. But the role of the professional sales person is of course to sell products or services profitably.

Let's be realistic. This does not apply to charities or non-profit organizations, but in every other situation it is the responsibility of everyone in the business to make a profit. Isn't it therefore rather strange that 'profit' has become a dirty word? There are of course some organizations that make outrageous profits, but they really are in the minority. The vast majority of businesses are striving to make a more modest profit. Profit to me is a good word. It creates job security. It provides an opportunity for employees to enhance their own standard of living. Profit also means money for research and development, and wise business owners retain some of that profit for the tough times which unfortunately face us all (although we are never quite sure when).

When I first started in business there were some 750,000 sales people employed selling financial products. Today there are less than 100,000. There are many reasons that there are fewer people employed in selling, but it is primarily because of the high cost of employment and of course the internet.

With the high cost of employment and the great difficulty in finding really successful sales people to employ, the task of winning new business has fallen back on to business owners. Numerous professionals now also have the task of winning new clients. Most of these people have had little or no training on how or what to do, and naturally have an abhorrence of adopting high-pressure foot-in-the-door hard sales tactics. These professionals did not spend years qualifying to become sales people. So here lies the dichotomy: they know it is very important to win new clients, but somehow just don't 'have the time' or will find any plausible excuse not to do it.

Let's get real. Winning new business is a must. It can also be fun, it is very rewarding and it is really very easy as long as you know how and are prepared to have a go.

All I ask you to do at this stage is to have an open mind and a willingness to accept the responsibility. Take a positive attitude of learning, rather than making excuses for non-participation and/or depending on others.

'The customer pays the wages' is a well-known cliché, but it is very useful to remind ourselves and the others we work with of this saying. If you want to get paid, what are you doing to win new customers? What are you doing to retain your existing customers?

I obviously don't know what time of day you are reading this book, but let me assure you categorically: there is someone out there right now either calling on or planning to call on your clients. Right now you have competition attempting to persuade your existing clients to switch their business or allegiance, just as you will try to persuade others to do business with your organization. Let me challenge you. Do you really deserve to keep your existing clients and customers? Don't expect them to be loyal. Loyalty cannot be demanded or expected, and is only earned by the hour or day. We shall cover in more detail how to retain your existing client base in Chapter 11.

Here is a question worthwhile asking yourself regularly. What business are you in? I recall asking a very successful publisher this question a number of years ago. He replied, 'You know what business I'm in. We publish books.' My reply was, 'Yes, of course you are right, but that is just the process. You are really in the business of selling books.' Let's be realistic and keep everything in perspective. There are countless thousands of publishers, but only the successful ones have the skill and willingness to adopt a sales and marketing culture.

We have all heard the cliché 'Good products sell themselves.' We all know this is emphatically not true. I have never seen a good product selling itself. History is littered with incredible inventions that have never made it to the marketplace. James Dyson invented the first bagless vacuum cleaner. It had superior cleaning power to every model in the marketplace. It was nearly 12 years before he was able to raise the funding needed for the sales and marketing activity to get it off the ground. The rest is history. The Dyson cleaner became a worldwide product and took a massive market share.

Sadly, too many business people dislike actively winning business. In other words, they don't like selling. They convince themselves that the answer is to advertise, then sit back and wait for the post, or for the phone to ring. I can assure you that they will be added to the list of business failures. True, some advertising does work, but as the great Henry Ford of the Ford Motor Company said, 'Fifty per cent of my advertising works. I only wish I knew which 50 per cent.' Most businesses find that direct response advertising rather than awareness advertising is effective.

For the smaller to medium-size enterprises, awareness advertising cannot be justified as cost-effective. Therefore, to be really successful and secure the future of your business, you must be proactive. In other words, you must be willing to go out, find and meet new prospective customers. Please don't go broke waiting for the phone call or the mail to arrive.

No doubt you have a picture in your mind of a successful business winner, and perhaps you are completely right. But there is one aspect I wish to clarify in helping you to develop a truly successful image. For too long there has been a belief that successful business winners have to be pushy. Let me ask you, do you like to buy from a pushy person? Do you want to do business with a pushy person? Of course you don't. So really the pushy person is not a successful business winner.

The business winner is the opposite of that. The successful business winner is a 'pully' person. Your prospects, customers and clients should want to take your call. They should look forward to meeting you. When you leave their company, they should be thinking they are really glad to have seen you. When you are walking down the high street and they see you coming in the opposite direction, they should not want to dive into the first shop to avoid meeting you. It is so much easier to be a pully person than a pushy one. This is covered in more detail in Chapter 3.

The vast majority of us really don't like being sold to, but we do like buying. Yet when we are buying and it is an enjoyable experience, it is nearly always as a result of an excellent inter-personal relationship. Think of the times when you have made purchases yourself, possibly in a retail outlet, and you have been handled by an expertly trained and knowledgeable assistant. He or she was really enabling you to make a decision. Again let me generalize. Most of us don't like making decisions, almost certainly because they could be the wrong ones. Again in most cases, having made a decision to purchase, we then experience post-purchase remorse.

Imagine going into a retailer and buying a new plasma screen television. Having made the purchase we will then quite understandably think of reasons we should not have bought it, or could have bought better. We may even look for price comparisons in other retailers or online. So business winners can often be described as 'mind maker-uppers'. In other words, they help people to buy well, to make up their minds by giving them all the necessary information that enables them to justify their purchase when the remorse sets in. Thank goodness these days the customer is protected from shoddy sales tactics, because people are allowed a cooling-off period and are covered by legislation. They can return a product or not pay for a service that is not correctly delivered.

I have been passionate about this subject for many years, and am determined my clients will never run any risk by trading with the Richard Denny Group and my brand. We carry the risk on every transaction. I am sure that you have noticed that on the back cover of this book there is a money-back guarantee. You have been graceful enough to invest in yourself by purchasing this book. I know there is no risk for you because if you follow the unfolding techniques you will win new clients and new business. Throughout this book every idea and concept has been practised thousands of times by winners. My risk is that you may not choose to follow the advice! What is the old saying? 'You can take a horse to water but you can't make it drink.'

So now I challenge you and your business. Do you offer your customers a 100 per cent money-back guarantee? If not, why not? Whenever I have asked that question, the reply is nearly always something along the lines, 'We might get taken for a ride.' Yes there is a very small risk here. Marks & Spencer became one of the most successful retailers in the world because it was the first to offer a 100 per cent refund, and continues to do so to this day. I am sure that over the years that a minority of people have bought clothes on a Saturday, worn them on Saturday night and returned them on the Monday. Of course M&S has been ripped off. But as a counterbalance millions have gone to M&S and bought two or three items more, and never returned them.

If you really want to get ahead of the competition, create a system with either a money-back guarantee or guaranteed satisfaction, whereby your client has no risk whatsoever in trading with you. This is called risk reversal. I have never heard of a business going to the wall because it guaranteed its products or services.

So what's at stake? Your destiny really is in your control. If you want to rise to the top in a professional equity partnership, you will get there faster and be wealthier if you are willing and able to enthusiastically embrace the activity of winning new clients. If you are a business owner the choice is yours: either pack up now and prevent a long-drawn-out, miserable and painful existence, or immediately start to become an enthusiastic proactive business winner. The future of your business is not with tweaking the product or service, but in finding and keeping new customers.

Pocket Reminders

■ Nothing happens anywhere in the world until a sale takes place.
■ You will lose some clients every year.
■ The customer pays the wages.
■ Right now somebody could be approaching your clients to persuade them to move.
■ What business are you in?
■ Be a pully person, not a pushy person.
■ How about risk reversal?

Wise words

If you are constantly looking back, chances are you will fall into a hole ahead.

2

The Quick Wins

You are no doubt reading this book in order to get some inspiration and learn techniques to win new business quickly and easily. So let's establish a little reality. There is far too much mystery surrounding successful business tactics. I personally believe we are trapped in a business culture that is becoming too sophisticated by far, impeding the most simple and common-sense way forward. For example, email is of course an outstanding technological advance, but it has now become the world's biggest time waster. Used with common sense, wisely and sparingly, it is an excellent tool of communication, but sadly this is not the norm.

Some new trend is forever being created in the business environment, such as neurolinguistic programming (NLP) and emotional intelligence. Each one is sold as the all-important solution to greater achievement. There is of course some value in these ideas, but it is limited. Most of these concepts are based on basic principles that have been around for years, but have been given a new label. One of the first mnemonics I ever learnt for a rule about how to be a success in life was KISS (keep it simple, stupid). So as this book unfolds you'll find it really is back to basics. Let's not complicate the great principles that really do work.

Let's get started right now with some basics. There are only four ways to grow a business. There are of course numerous ways of making profits but only *four* ways to grow a business. I repeat this intentionally, as it must become second nature, and should be shared with everyone that you work with. I cannot stress this enough, as it will be the foundation for your future success, whatever business you are in.

The four ways are:

▇ increasing the number of customers;
▇ increasing the average transaction value;
▇ increasing the frequency of repurchase;
▇ acquisition.

If these appear to be common sense, so much the better.

Increasing the number of customers

Increasing your number of customers is, of course, what the majority of this book will be guiding you through. Be sure of one aspect: any business that is not actively getting new customers will sooner or later go bust. The law of attrition states that you will lose a percentage of your customers every year, however effective your products or services are, however well they are priced, and however good your customer care is, because people move away, they die, or they change to a competitor. This is known as circumstantial change.

Increasing the average transaction value

Increasing the average transaction value is a massive opportunity for most businesses. Sadly it is an area that is not fully understood, and often neglected. It is rarely even measured. What is your average customer spend? Let me give you an example. The average customer spend in a big UK supermarket is currently £76.00. The average customer spend in a small corner shop is £8.40. So for example, where the owner places the sandwiches in the small shop could be crucial. Ideally they should be at the back of the shop, so the customer not only buys a sandwich, but makes other impulse purchases on the way to the till. If the average customer spend can be increased by £1 per customer, the retailer will seriously increase its profitability. In most businesses there are products or services that customers have not been offered, but would willingly purchase if only they knew about them.

Let me tell you a story. A short while ago I was asked to do some business training for my then accountants. My brief was to help the partners win new clients. This firm audited our books, so I concentrated on helping it to win more audit work. While I was doing this one of the partners said, 'Richard, we don't just do auditing. We have a payroll service, and we do computer-based training.' He then proceeded to tell me of approximately 20 other services (products) that they had to offer. I said, 'I didn't know you have a payroll service. If I had known we would have used you. We have another company taking care of that for us.' The partner replied, 'We did tell you.' I countered, 'No, you didn't.' He then responded, 'Yes, we did.'

Anyhow, enough of the Punch and Judy. I asked the staff, 'How did you tell me?' They said, 'We sent you a brochure.' I confessed, 'You know where that went.' If only they had bothered to speak to me and mention the service, I would immediately have given them the payroll business. Apart from anything else, we would have saved some money, and the services we used would all have been under one umbrella. This is a classic example of what so many professionals do: fail to communicate effectively with their clients.

Let me give you another example. I have another client that manufactures lifts. Its main profit comes not from the core product but from the add-ons, and more particularly the after-sales service and maintenance contracts. A final example is a major furniture retailer that I worked with, helping it to have the latest and most professional sales people in the United Kingdom. The major contribution to profit came from the sale of Scotchgard™ fabric protector, and finance for purchases, and not from the furniture itself.

Please now look at Table 2.1, which shows a sample sales matrix. Then use it as a basis to compile your own. This is a very basic example of a banking matrix.

It is a well-known fact that when a customer or client buys more than one product from a single supplier, it is more likely to stay with that supplier. Banks have found that where clients purchase a number of what they call services (which in reality are products), they are overwhelmingly more likely to stay. Of course, the client also becomes much more profitable.

The financial industry is without question the most competitive. Most of us have up to 40 offers a year to take out a new credit card or to switch our allegiance from one bank to another. Banks particularly have discovered that they have a much higher retention rate with customers who use a greater number of their products, because there appears to be too much hassle involved in switching to another bank. But it is very easy to switch if the relationship is less complicated. I also have to say that in most cases it is in your own customers' best interests to buy more products and services from you. So this is, like all good business practice, a win–win situation.

We all know that it is much easier to sell and do business with an existing customer than find a new one. If you or your company have been in business for more than a year, you must have an existing client/customer base. Ask yourself, how many

Table 2.1 Sales matrix for a bank

Products or Services

Customer /client account name	Current account	Loan account	Savings card	Credit	Mortgage insurance	Home insurance	Life insurance	Contents	Pension
R C Clarke	✔		✔	✔	✔				
B W Sparling	✔		✔	✔					
A W Thompson	✔		✔						

of your customers are using all your products and services? If not, why not?

Let me say it again. It is in your existing customers' best interests to do business with you. More than likely they really are unaware of all you have to offer. You see, it's not their job. They have to concentrate on their business. It is your job to inform them of what you can do for them. I find it particularly frustrating trying to explain this to professional service providers, as they seem to work with an 'island' mentality. Let me explain. Most are specialists in a given field within the broader scope of the business. They think of themselves as 'owning' their clients, and fail to introduce them to the firm's other partners and/or specialities. I must also stress that it appears many of them have an inherent fear of sharing clients with other partners. In some cases they feel that their clients might be let down. It is of course a little bit scary when people show such a lack of trust in their colleagues. But in the vast majority of situations I have come across, the real problem lies in the fact that the professional doesn't want to appear to be pushy. Certainly many professionals feel it is beneath them to give the impression that they might be selling.

So if you work in a professional services organization, I challenge you now. How many of your existing contacts are using other services from your firm? I must really challenge you on this, as in my opinion if they are not, you are not only not looking after your colleagues' best interests, you also might not be looking after your clients' best interests. Let me give you a simple example of a law firm. The general public most commonly use a solicitor for property conveyancing. If you are a property specialist and new clients come to you, isn't this a golden opportunity to demonstrate care for your clients by introducing them to other partners who could also help them? Maybe a colleague could make or update a client's will, or maybe you could introduce him or her to a financial specialist who would provide useful pensions advice. Maybe the client owns a business, and could be introduced to the corporate department. It really is just a simple mind-set change: from island thinking to lateral thought. Just start to think about your clients and their needs and lifestyles. This simple example can apply right across the board to many other professions.

Similarly, if you are a business person, have customers buying your products been offered a maintenance agreement or service contract? We have a brilliant stationery supplier who is a joy to deal with. When we phone in to place an order, the telephonists are extremely well trained. Again, let me illustrate with a simple example. We phone in to place an order for reams of paper. The telephonist says, 'Are you all right for ink cartridges? And did you know we are doing a special offer on envelopes this month?' It is so easy to forget to offer these extras, and it is so gratifying when our suppliers demonstrate that they care about our business. The cynics among you will now be smirking, 'Oh yes, they are trying to sell to you.' Of course they are – but isn't it a joy to be sold to well?

So here is the easy way to increase the average transaction value: sell the *add-on*. Let's suppose you are in conversation on the telephone with a customer. When you have nearly completed the main business, you can drop in a phrase like this:

> Just while you're on the line, I don't know if I mentioned that we also do …

> Just while you're on the line, I noticed that you haven't ordered…

> Just while you're on the line, it occurs to me you may need…

In other situations you will have scheduled meetings with your client or customer. Prior to your meeting, always decide which add-on service you are going to promote. Remember that one of the golden rules of professional selling is to sell only one product or service at a time. Get a decision and then move on. Then offer another service on your next phone call or meeting.

You could introduce the subject by saying:

By the way, did you know...?

Incidentally, we also...

I forgot to tell you about...

Did you know...

I was thinking of you and thought you might be interested to know...

You may not be aware...

Increasing the frequency of repurchase

Let me explain what this really means. If customers do business with you once a year, what could you do to enable them to do business with you twice a year? If customers trade with you once a month, what could you do to increase that to once every two weeks? The objective of this opportunity in growing your business is to shorten the purchase trading cycle. And what this really means is that once you have won new customers, you need to keep them.

I am amazed how bad businesses generally are at customer retention. Huge sums of money are spent on advertising, promotion, marketing, public relations, brochure design, the employment of sales people and so on, with the sole purpose of winning new customers. Then it seems companies pass those customers over to the business prevention department. They dream up new ways and processes to frustrate and upset clients, and eventually lose them to a competitor. I will state to you right now, the single biggest opportunity to become out-standingly successful is through customer care via a customer relationship management (CRM) programme. All about this will be revealed in Chapter 12.

Acquisition

I am not an authority on the buying or selling of businesses and companies, so I shall not give guidance on how to proceed successfully with this activity. If at any stage this becomes your responsibility, there are other people, books and programmes that I am sure will give you sound advice. May I recommend the Institute of Directors, Pall Mall, London, as a first port of call.

There is so much at stake for you and your business by increasing your average transaction value. There is so much profit at stake. So let me be emphatic: please don't be a weak streak of … and think that you can achieve the same result by email or a brochure as you can by speaking to people directly – unless of course you are determined to go broke. Please speak to people.

The second mnemonic I learnt as a 20 year old was taught to me by Barry Wells, a very successful business manager. 'Richard,' he said, 'if you never want to go broke just remember to keep TTPing.' Of course I asked, 'What does that stand for?' He said, 'Talking to people.' In emphasizing the importance of TTP, let me ask you, what is the worst thing that could happen if you give a customer a call? In reality the worst possible outcome is that your customer might say 'No thank you', or 'I'll bear that in mind.' That's not too painful, is it, really?

In my own experience and that of my numerous clients, I have never known anyone to lose a customer by offering another product or service. In many, many cases the client will not give an immediate yes, but he or she might come back for that product or service in the weeks or months ahead, and in most cases will be very grateful for your suggestion.

Price increase

This is another 'quick win', and again I must ask you to be open-minded and not reject this concept. Before I unfold the idea, may I remind you that you are in business to make a profit. Of course this has to be done in an honest and ethical way. This activity could also come under the heading of increasing your average transaction value, but I want to treat it as a separate entity because it is so important.

Let me commence with a question. When was the last time you increased your prices? It may have been only a few weeks ago. But in my experience and consultancy, most of my clients have not revised their prices for at least a year, and sometimes for four years. There seems to be a massive fear surrounding an increase in prices. People believe the business will lose a lot of its customers. Again, let's be realistic. We are all working in a very competitive marketplace, and of course in order to survive you must be competitive, but there is a balance to be struck. You need to keep and if possible improve on your profitability, without driving your customers away.

I can categorically assure you that my suggestions have been adopted by countless numbers of my clients, and have proved exceptionally successful. Let me give you just one example. One of my clients is an optician with a number of outlets. As I am sure you are aware, this is a very competitive field. No doubt you have seen national advertising campaigns inviting people to buy one pair of spectacles and get one pair free. My client had not had a price increase for some 18 months. It was considering a 2 per cent increase across the board. It had a range of approximately 70 different products, not including spectacles, where there were in excess of 300 styles.

The average cost of frames was approximately £70. After much deliberation the client suggested to me that these too should be subject to a 2 per cent increase. On the frames alone this would have meant an average increase of only £1.40. This would hardly be worth the effort of drawing up new price lists. I suggested to my client that in the vast majority of cases frames are not a price-sensitive purchase. People will always find the money for what they want. On a purchase price of £70, I suggested the client could at least look for an increase of £5. As we discussed this in more detail, it turned out that a 10 per cent increase on all the products and services would hardly be noticed from the customers' perspective. The result was that my client took the bull by the horns, and with great courage it implemented the 10 per cent increase. I advised the firm exactly how to handle it.

The first point to make is the big No No. This is what you must not do. When a customer asks how much a product is, the optometrist and/or technician must not reply saying, 'I'm afraid we've had a price increase,' or 'I'm so sorry, but the price has gone up.' The response must be positive: for instance, 'Those frames are £75.20.' In other words, just state the price. The optician implemented the increase, did not lose a single customer, and the increased income has made a great contribution to the security of the business.

So whenever you increase your prices or fees, please, please do not contact your customers with a grovelling apology. At a given date, just put up the prices or fees. If you are quoting a price or fee, now or in the future, preface the amount with something like this:

I have some good news for you. The price is...

This is good value at...

I am pleased to say...

Our fee rate is...

I said earlier that business must be honest and ethical. Under no circumstances should you mislead your client or customer. I find it despicable when customers are given the impression they are buying at a given price, and when the invoice arrives it is at a higher rate. If you are currently taking orders, always confirm the price, even if as a last resort you have to say 'Our current price is...'

The less you are concerned about your prices or fees, the less your customers will be. We shall go into a little more detail on this subject in Chapter 10.

I have found through feedback from my clients that this has truly been a quick win for making their businesses more profitable. In the worst-case scenario, from information provided to me by clients over a large cross-section of industries, one client told me that it had lost 2 per cent of its customers. It was probably going to lose them anyway, and the increase in profitability surpassed the small loss to the customer base.

Let's keep our feet in the real world. Don't be greedy and think that you can get away with a massive hike. Nor should you base your increase on a simple percentage. If your average product cost is £10 you might only wish to increase it to £10.85. If your average hourly rate is £270.00 you might increase it to £275.00 or even £278.00.

Let's look at an example. Say you increase your firm's hourly rate by £5.

If you have 40 billing hours per week, 40 × £5 = £200 weekly increase in income.

If you work for 45 billable weeks per year, 45 × £200 = £9,000 annual increase in income.

For each billable member of staff – you can do this calculation.

That figure of £9,000 even for one person goes straight to the bottom line of your profit and loss account. You are now working well and increasing your profits.

May I suggest that 98 per cent of your clients are not going to go away if they can buy a similar service for £5 per hour cheaper.

Here are a few further ideas for quickly attracting new customers, particularly if you have spare capacity.

Free trial

It has been proven many times that offering a free trial on a product, and certainly on a service, will attract some new customers. It is up to you then to make that trial so successful that the prospective client cannot resist doing business with you in future. The free trial can be offered in a little brochure or letter targeted at those customers or clients you really wish to attract, and should be followed up with a courtesy call. The 'how tos' are covered in Chapter 6.

Barter

Have you ever considered bartering some of your business activities with a supplier? One very successful organization specializes in helping businesses to trade using an original business exchange system. It is becoming more and more popular, and even some of the multinationals are using this very convenient method of trading. Bartercard is currently the world leader, and can be contacted via its website, uk.bartercard.com.

A voucher

This is of course not suitable for all businesses, but it is very usable in certain industries, and with some imagination can be used in many fields. A hairdresser could offer a £10 voucher to be used on the first appointment. A law firm could offer a £20 voucher towards the making of a will. Vouchers should always be in monetary value and never as a percentage off. Percentages are not tangible, but a monetary voucher is tangible, and is less likely to be thrown away. Let's face it, people understand money.

Incentives for existing clients

If you are considering a sale, your clients should be invited to a preview before it is opened to the general public. Incentives can be offered to your existing customers, again with imagination. They will demonstrate care and value.

Pocket Reminders

- There are only four ways to grow a business.
- Build a sales matrix and work it out now.
- How about a price increase?
- Contact your existing customers.
- Be honest and ethical.
- Offer a free trial.

Wise words

Describe your product in terms of what it 'does' not in terms of what it 'is'.

3

Walk a Mile in My Shoes

Many of us living today are caught up in the culture of self-gratification. People spend too much time thinking about themselves – their wants – their needs – their pressures – their illnesses – their money – their relationships and their success. Many feel the world owes them something, and that their rights are all-important. People get married and then adopt a behavioural style of 'make me happy'. If only they realized that by making their partner happy they in turn would find so much joy and fulfilment. In the words of the American singer and song writer Sheryl Crow, 'It's not having what you want, it's wanting what you have.'

Likewise in commerce, business people are wrapped up in themselves. They have targets to achieve. They have budgets to keep, and have to perform to their boss's expectation and, for some, the demands of their shareholders. All this manifests itself in a 'drive and strive' mentality. My favourite word must now be dropped in – 'balance'. Of course there is nothing wrong with targets and budgets and striving to achieve other people's expectations, but many people are missing a simple trick, because there is a faster and more certain route to success and achievement.

There is a marvellous song that was written and recorded by Joe South in 1969, 'Walk a mile in my shoes.' The opening lyrics are:

'If I could be you and you could be me for just one hour

If we could find a way to get inside each other's minds

If you could see me through my eyes instead of your ego

I believe you'd be surprised to see that you've been blind

Walk a mile in my shoes.'

As the song says, the simple trick is to step into your prospect's shoes from time to time. You need to develop a passionate desire to help him or her to greater achievement, happiness or fulfilment, and in the process satisfy his or her wants and needs.

So if you truly desire to become more successful in business, I ask you now to check your mindset. This is fundamental to being a modern, successful and *happy* business winner. We all know there is only one certainty: you have got to live with yourself for the rest of your life. Do you want to live with you as you are for the rest of your life? Sadly I come across too many people who have real difficulties with themselves and their past. We cannot change one nanosecond of yesterday, last week, last month or indeed any of our past. We can, however, have a major impact on the next hour, next week and next year.

Being a successful business winner does not have to mean you must be unethical, abrasive, aggressive or ruthless. Those who wish to get to the top do not need to trample others on the way. I can assure you that this is not and never will be the route to long-term happiness and to being able to live with yourself.

A real winner understands and practises empathy, but be aware that there is a balance to be struck. It is very easy to be trapped into a situation of seeing the other person's point of view so well that you lose all ability and usefulness. So much dysfunctionality is caused by the extremes. Virtually all of the world's strife has a root in extremism, and unfortunately one of the great tragedies is the loss of balance and common sense.

We must be able to step into the other person's shoes and then back into our own. We can spend time truly understanding our client's, customer's and our prospect's world, but should not live it. The role of the business winner is of course a role of persuasion, and with that in mind you need to be plausible and convincing. If we follow the theme of seeing the world from the other person's perspective, let me ask you, what sort of person would you like, or do you like, to do business with?

I am going to build a picture of the personality that appeals to me. I might add that it has, in my experience, the characteristics of the most successful business winners. Now as I build this profile, please don't think of the exception to the rule. At the moment the programme *The Apprentice* is on television, presented by Sir Alan Sugar. It has received acclaim as well as criticism. As we all know, this programme is designed for entertainment. The behaviour of Sir Alan and some of the participants is really not conducive to success in the real world.

Here is a list of attractive characteristics of business winners:

■ trustworthy;
■ honest;
■ enthusiastic;
■ positive;
■ happy;
■ a 'pully' sort of person;
■ knowledgeable;

■ quietly ambitious;
■ principled;
■ helpful;
■ caring;
■ a people person.

Please add some of your own.

Just as importantly, we must identify some of the traits of people we don't want to do business with. Here is a list of some of my dislikes:

■ pushy;
■ shifty;
■ fast talking;
■ gimmicky;
■ slick;
■ unconfident;
■ smarmy;
■ egotistical;
■ creepy;
■ over familiar;
■ too full of themselves;
■ dishonest;
■ greedy.

Please add your own dislikes to this list.

Now let's compile a list of behavioural characteristics with likes and dislikes. Let's start with the likes. Most of us like people who:

■ are really interested in us;
■ look us in the eye;
■ recall our name and something about us;
■ recall details of a previous conversation;
■ really listen to our every word;

▧ while they are with us, treat us as the most important person;

▧ when they don't know something, say that they don't.

These are some dislikes:

▧ trying to sell us something we don't want or need;

▧ talking too much about themselves;

▧ can't make eye contact with us;

▧ interrupting while we are speaking;

▧ in love with their own product, service and themselves.

Now please take a few minutes and gain from past experience. Think about people that you have bought from or done business with, and add to the few examples listed above from your own experience. Think about the times you really enjoyed a transaction or business experience. Then think about the occasions when you may have liked the product or service, but couldn't stand the person you were communicating with.

I'm not asking you to change your personality, but what I am saying is that if you have the responsibility of winning business, you should at least make an effort to become the sort of person that you would like to do business with.

I hope and trust that the vast majority of the readers of this book regard themselves as professionals. Many of you will be communicating with other professionals, often in the business to business (B2B) world rather than the business to consumer (B2C) world. With this in mind, these are the behavioural traits that often require a little bit of effort if you want to become the successful business winner.

> I want to deal with people that do not waste my time and get to the point.

Your prospects' time is just as valuable as yours. They are not interested and do not have time for small talk with possibly a complete stranger. In the majority of cases they know exactly why you are there. So tell them – you are hoping to do some business with them and you are hoping to earn the privilege of doing so. Let me illustrate this point with a recent experience.

I was approached by Gordon Patterson of Franchise Development Services. The purpose of the meeting was to ascertain whether my company's activities would be suitable for franchising. Gordon arrived and did the normal polite British small talk of weather and travel, then got straight to the point. He explained in a few sentences his company's areas of expertise, what it does for its clients, and most interestingly the results it has achieved for its clients. He said that to save a lot of time further down the line, he would like to get a full understanding of my business. He proceeded to ask some very informed questions. As this progressed, it became evident that he knew his subject and he had done his research: he had looked at our website and so on. When he had gained a full understanding of our business, he then outlined a very constructive, no-risk plan for us to commence the franchising process.

He was well aware of our timing: I had made it clear we were not currently considering franchising, and that the timescale from our side could well be up to five years. He left that meeting with a promise to provide us with a staged proposal and development strategy, but most importantly of all, my co-director and I both felt that this was a person with whom we could definitely do business. In hindsight perhaps what was most comforting was the feeling he gave us that the process would be relatively painless.

In Laurie Mellor's book *Sales Success in Tough Times* (2003), he states, 'empathy is the jewel in the crown of emotional intelligence'. Empathy requires us to read other people's emotions, their unspoken feelings. This is epitomized by reading their body language (a subject covered in more detail in Chapter 5). In developing your own skill of reading body language, just take time out to observe other people.

Let me give you a very simple example. When I am interviewing people for a vacancy I try to watch them from the moment of their arrival. How do they get out of the car? How do they walk into the building? We can all interpret a person's walk. Are they purposeful? Are they confident? Are they exhibiting drive and importance?

I said in Chapter 2 that one of the trends in business today is the importance of emotional intelligence. Daniel Goleman, probably the most respected authority on the subject, states in his book *Emotional Intelligence* (1996), 'the rules for work are changing. They take for granted intellectual ability and technical know-how and instead focus on personal qualities, such as empathy, initiative, adaptability and persuasiveness. This is no passing fad.' I personally believe that the need for those qualities is certainly not a passing fad. They have always been and always will be part of the criteria for business achievement as well as general happiness. I have more difficulty with the fact that this has been wrapped with the emotional intelligence concept. The idea that the ways in which people organize themselves and relate to others are important is not new at all.

Emotional intelligence is about what it says it is: intelligently managing our emotions. Emotional unintelligence would imply giving free rein to feelings and emotions. On the other hand, emotional intelligence manages those feelings so that they are expressed effectively and appropriately, and achieve the desired response or reaction rather than the undesired one.

I asked you the question, what sort of person do you like to do business with? Now ask yourself the question, are you that sort of person? Because *this* is in your control.

When I started my career in business the first book I read was Dale Carnegie's *How to Win Friends and Influence People* (1953). The book was written in the 1930s and is still in print today, with millions of copies sold worldwide. I consider this book to be possibly the greatest self-help book ever to be written. In part 2 there is a section entitled 'Six ways to make people like you.' I refer to this for no other reason than that business really is all about our interaction with people. The first tablet of stone taught to aspiring sales professionals is the saying, 'people buy people'. We all realize that we are more likely to do business with a person we like than with one we dislike. I have already stated that our prospective customers have massive choice. We all face increased competition. More than ever before it is crucial that every one of us tasked with winning more business remembers that tablet of stone.

Very rarely is your product or service the only one available, but if your clients really enjoy your company they are more likely to have dealings with you, even if there is a better offer from a competitor. In all honesty, it is much easier to be a nice person, a trusted person than to always have the best product or service in the marketplace.

You don't have to change your personality, but you have to develop personally, and from time to time step into your prospects' shoes – get inside their minds – see through their eyes. This will go an immeasurable way in helping you to become a person whom people will want to do business with.

Pocket Reminders

- ■ Be a people person.
- ■ Do you have compassion?
- ■ Would you want to buy from yourself?
- ■ Build your own understanding of empathy.
- ■ Step out of your shoes regularly.

Wise words

Attitudes are contagious. Is yours worth catching?

4

Seize the Day

Our most valuable asset is not our house or any of our possessions or our bank account. It is of course our brain and our mind. Everything that we do and achieve is dependent on this amazing bit of kit. Fascinatingly the majority of people really do not value or take sufficient care of their brain and state of mind. You know as well as I that when you are feeling positive, almost anything can be achieved. On the other hand if you are feeling negative, virtually nothing worthwhile can be achieved.

The majority of people take better care of their car than they do their brain. They spend a great deal of money to make sure that their car runs smoothly and doesn't let them down. Cars require regular servicing and fuel to function. I make this simple analogy because in order to be truly successful in business the brain also needs care and attention. It needs a little investment from time to time. It needs oxygen from regular exercise. It needs new ideas, which can come from reading or learning from others. But you must accept that a positive attitude is the major ingredient of winning.

One of the laws of success states that it is desire, not ability, that determines our success. I was brought up to believe that success was dependent on ability. I have since discovered that without question this is not the case. It is overwhelmingly dependent on desire. If we want to do something desperately enough, we will gain the ability. Here is one very small example.

The British television programme *Top Gear* has been running a little competition for all manner of celebrities to test their skills driving around a race track in a standard family car. Over 50 people have taken part over the years. In 2006 Ellen MacArthur, the young yachtswoman who holds the world record for sailing around the world single-handedly, was given the opportunity to have a drive. The programme showed her driving. She was not happy with her first circuit. She pleaded to have another try but this was not allowed. Ellen was interviewed prior to her lap time being announced, and she explained to the presenter Jeremy Clarkson that she really wanted another chance as she felt she could do better. She does very little driving, she explained, because she is at sea for at least six months a year. She was almost apologetic about her lack of motoring experience. Clarkson then announced her time, and she went straight to the top of the leader board. The film of her driving was shown, and the intensity of concentration and her determination to win were extremely evident. This simple example reinforced my belief that if we want to do something strongly, we can. The brain is our most valuable asset.

Take care of yours and nourish it. Your brain has infinite capacity and untapped potential. But this chapter is not so much about your most valuable asset, as it is about your most valuable resource. This is a bank account that we all have in common, but it is an account with peculiarities.

You cannot deposit into it. You can only withdraw. There is no statement telling you how much you have left in it. It is of course the bank account of time. So seize the day.

There are those who make things happen.

There are those who watch things happen.

And:

There are those who wonder what happened.

The most common reason (for this, read excuse) for not doing something is, 'I haven't had the time.' Let's imagine a man receives a letter from a lawyer, stating that a distant relative has left him £2 million. The lawyer requests the recipient to telephone on receipt of the letter, and make an appointment to come into the office to sign the necessary documents so the money can be transferred into his bank account. I guarantee he would find the time.

You see, in reality getting things done is all about priority. We have a natural tendency to do the things we enjoy, rather than things that may be more important.

There are numerous books and courses on the subject of time management, and of course they are extremely helpful. But as a matter of fact it is impossible to manage time so as to fit everything in. There are only 24 hours in a day and 365 days in a year. We can only choose what we do in the time available, and none of us truly know how much time we have left.

There is a lot of talk today about work–life balance, and rightly so, as we are living in a culture of pressure to perform, to meet others' expectations and to work longer and longer hours. I am convinced that a person's last thought as he or she departs this world will never be, 'I wish I had spent more time at the office.'

Let me share with you a story sent to me by my sister-in-law, Stacy Saunders. A professor was holding a philosophy class. He had a glass jar, and proceeded to fill it with golf balls. He asked the students whether the jar was full, and they agreed it was. He then picked up a small box of pebbles and poured them into the jar. The professor gave the jar a shake, and the pebbles rolled into the gaps between the golf balls. He again asked the students whether the jar was full, and they agreed it was. Next he poured sand into the jar, and of course there was plenty of space for it to fill. Once more he asked the question, is the jar full now? The students responded with an unanimous yes. The professor then produced two cups of coffee and poured the entire contents into the jar. 'Now,' said the professor as the laughter subsided, 'I want you to recognize that this jar represents your life. The golf balls are the important things – your family, your children, your health, your friends and the things you hold dear. If everything else was lost and only they remained, your life would still be full.

'The pebbles are the other things that matter, like your job, your house and perhaps your car. The sand is everything else – the small stuff. If you put the sand into the jar first, there is no room for the pebbles or the golf balls. The same goes for life. If you spend all your time and energy on the small stuff, you will never have room for the things that are really important to you.'

One of the students asked what the coffee represented. The professor smiled and replied, 'I'm glad you asked. It just goes to show you that no matter how full your life may seem, there's always room for a couple of cups of coffee with a friend.'

If we are really fortunate, our life is divided three ways. One third is work. One third is play (evenings, weekends, holidays and retirement). One third is spent sleeping. The purpose of the one third spent at work is to make sure that the one third at play can give us the things in life that we would like to enjoy, and of course our happiness. And I might add that it isn't amazing to learn that if we are happy in our work, we are much more likely to be happy at play.

While we are discussing time and balance, it is worthwhile mentioning stress. Realistically stress can be good if it is managed. Stress can help us to be more creative – rise higher, jump farther and achieve more. When it is not managed it can make us seriously ill, requiring expert treatment. The three biggest causes of stress at work needing medical attention are:

■ mismanagement of time;
■ people being asked to do a new job and not being trained to do it;
■ sheer work overload with appraisal only once a year: this is rare in the private sector but very common in the public sector.

Now let's establish some parameters. There is an enormous difference between individuals in activity and achievement. A person can be very busy all day without actually achieving very much. This sort of person arrives home at the end of the working day mentally and physically exhausted, with little to show for his or her efforts. Such people suffer from the human frailty of procrastination. They put things off that they should be doing immediately.

On the other hand, people can be very busy all day actually ticking off items from their 'to do' list, and at the end of the day they can see exactly what they have achieved.

A few years ago, Charles Schwab, who at that time was president of a US steel company, granted an interview to an efficiency expert named Ivy Lee. Lee was explaining his firm's services to Schwab. Schwab interrupted and said, 'That's all very well, but what we want is more doing, not knowing. We already know what should be done. If you can give me a programme to help me get more done in a day, I will pay you anything you ask.'

Lee replied, 'I'll give you a programme. You use it for 30

days and then get all of your key people to use it. Then send me a cheque for whatever you think it is worth.'

A few months later Lee received a cheque for $25,000, with a note from Schwab acknowledging that this was the finest lesson he had ever learnt. Five years later Schwab's company (the Bethlehem Steel Company) became the biggest steel corporation in the world. Charles Schwab became one of only two people at that time who were paid a salary of $1 million per year. The other man was Walter Chrysler, of car manufacturing fame.

As I am sure you have realized, this story relates to a few years ago. From Lee's original programme or system there eventually grew an industry on time management. The Filofax was created, and numerous other aids for getting more done in a day. Sadly, many of these current systems have so complicated the original concept that people find they need more time to manage the new whiz-bang time management programme.

Let me give you Lee's original concept, so simple yet so incredibly effective.

1. At the end of a day draw up a list of all the jobs you need to do the following day.
2. Now number them in their order of importance.
3. The following day when you start work, start at number one. Keep at it until it is complete, then move on to number two and keep at it until it's complete, and so on.

Let me now explain why one man who is no fool paid $25,000 for that idea. Most people do their 'to do' list first thing in the morning. For the majority of us this is when our brain is sharpest, and we should be doing rather than deciding what to do. If you are a manager, please always delegate the night before, and let your people plan their own days. There is nothing more frustrating for people at work than their boss continually interrupting their work in progress.

For you, the individual, planning your day the night before means that you can actively switch off in your private time. Lots of people make a 'to do' list, but they rarely manage the system very well. This is why it is so very important to prioritize.

Stage 3 on Lee's system says, start at number one and keep at it until the task is complete. In my experience the most important item is nearly always the most unpleasant. People generally have a tendency to do the things on their list that are easier or more enjoyable. But let's understand how our brain works. While you and I are doing those easier tasks, our brain knows that sooner or later we are going to have to tackle the unpleasant one. We are inclined to drag out the easier tasks, as our brain is dreading number one. On the other hand we all know that when we have dealt with an unpleasant task, we feel relieved and consequently more motivated. I have already said that your most valuable asset is your brain. Learn how to manage it better, as it is astonishing what it will do for you.

There will be many days when you have not completed the list. Do not worry. If you are using Lee's system there is no known way of getting more done in a day. Also remind yourself of one of the great laws of success. Seeing ourselves progressing motivates us. You will also see that every day becomes a day of achievement, not just a day of activity.

There is one further tip that is well worth bearing in mind. How do you decide in what order to prioritize your 'to do' list? This simple tip may not apply, but as someone who has the responsibility of (among other things) winning business, I have found it to be most effective. At the top of my list will always be an activity aimed at winning a new client or keeping an existing one. If we take our eye off that ball, we really are not promoting a winning culture.

Let's be realistic. I do not compile a 'to do' list every day, and neither need you. If I am away from the office on a speaking engagement, there is no point in making a 'to do' list of things I cannot possibly do that day. Why would I want to make my mind unhappy?

Happiness is a ticked-off 'to do' list.

Here are a few further ideas, as I am very conscious that many of my readers have the secondary responsibility of winning business, and a little planning will make this easier and more effective. Decide how many of these activities you want to do each month, then break the time down into weeks and days, and allocate a time for each activity:

■ introductory letters;
■ brochures to send out;
■ follow-up calls to make;
■ new appointments to make;
■ follow-up appointments to make;
■ cross-sell or up-sell conversations.

Please be realistic, as when you set those goals or targets they must be achievable.

Our resource of time is so precious that we all really must make a greater effort to maximize every day. There is a time to work and a time to play. Challenge yourself continually. Are you mixing the two? Let me give you an example. Many people at work spend too much time on coffee breaks, lunch breaks, unnecessary conversation with colleagues, playing on the internet, sending time-wasting emails, reading newspapers and magazines, and then they wonder why they haven't got all the things they had wanted to do completed in the day. And then we hear the excuse, 'I didn't have time.' If you want something done, ask a busy person.

Even though most businesses are becoming more electronic, there is still a mountain of paperwork to be dealt with. Many of my readers who run their own businesses also open their own mail. A worthwhile tip to strive for is to handle a piece of paper only once. It is so easy to open a letter, look at it, then move on to the rest of the mail. Without your even noticing, that paper can be handled half-a-dozen or more times before it is dealt with. What a waste of this resource – your precious bank account of time.

One of the major failings of executives is that they do not allow themselves the so-called 'luxury' of thinking time. This is not a luxury: it is paramount to achievement. Many people only have thinking time while in the car or travelling. I strongly recommend that setting aside quality thinking time becomes a priority. Give yourself perhaps only one or two hours a week when you can be out of contact, and are able to think and concentrate on your business. Let me reiterate: your most valuable asset is your brain. Give it a chance to be creative. It is staggering how it can solve problems and develop concepts, given the chance.

Here is another challenge. What do you do on the last two days before going on holiday? Research has shown that most people's work output in this period is phenomenal. Desks are cleared. In-trays are emptied. Decisions are taken. Outstanding emails are cleared. If we can do that on those days, in all honesty we can work like that every day of our lives.

Pocket Reminders

- ▓ Care for your most valuable asset.
- ▓ Are *you* stealing from your own bank account?
- ▓ Are you letting others steal from your bank account?
- ▓ Remember you can't manage time.
- ▓ Develop the habit of doing the daily easy 'to do' list.
- ▓ Happiness is a ticked off 'to do' list.

Wise words

The problem for many is not the absence of knowing what to do, but the absence of doing it.

5

The King's New Clothes

The popular family pantomime created by Bob Heather, *The King's New Clothes*, tells the story of King Cuthbert who is about to wed Princess Primrose from a neighbouring kingdom. He decides there would be nothing better than to have a brand new suit of clothes made for his wedding. He summons the royal tailors, but the suit they make is well below the expectations of the king. So he announces a competition to make a new suit for his wedding.

The king's evil brother, Baron Grumbleguts, thinks this is an ideal time to usurp his brother and take over the throne. He lures the gullible twins Tom and Jerry and their mother to make an 'invisible suit'. The plan is to make the king believe other people can see it. But it does not exist, and this realization is intended to humiliate the king to the point of abdication.

The pantomime develops this amusing theme. Eventually the king is conned into believing that the 'invisible suit' exists and is indeed beautiful. His close courtiers all lack the courage to tell him he is in fact naked.

I take this theme because so many people unfortunately don't have someone else to tell what they are really like. We rarely see ourselves as others do. Your marketplace is really all about people and their interactions. The image you have of yourself can be totally different from how other people see you.

I stated in Chapter 4 that if we are fortunate our life goes three ways, and the purpose of work is to create a lifestyle in our free time. And if we are more successful in our work, we are likely to become happier in our private life. Therefore if we have to dress or behave at work in a way that we would not normally do in our private life, so what? As long as the means achieve the ends, it's no problem.

We were all taught at some stage in our lives that first impressions count. We are all familiar with the cliché, 'Make a good first impression in order to develop a second.' Let me ask you again to step into the shoes of the people you would like to do business with. When they meet you the very first time, what do they expect to see?

Let's take the example of a farmer. A man calling at a farm to discuss, and with luck sell, a tractor would give completely the wrong impression if he were dressed in a pinstriped Savile Row suit. Likewise a person visiting an accountant for the first meeting would be taken aback if the accountant turned out to be wearing hip-hugging jeans and a cropped top. The advice here is to dress and conform to how your prospective customers would hope to see you.

Unfortunately in the United Kingdom there is a major problem in our hospitals with patients being abusive to hospital doctors (and other staff too). It is my belief that a lot of this could be reduced if only hospital doctors would dress as patients expect them to dress. This would build confidence in what the doctor says, and the treatment he or she prescribes. A very good friend of mine recently had major heart surgery, and told me the story of his hospital stay. He found it extremely worrying when medical staff visited him at his bedside. He could never distinguish between the junior doctors and the consultants. Richard didn't know how to address the staff, as none of them wore a simple name badge. He reckoned it would have been much easier if the junior doctors always wore a white coat with their name and the prefix 'Dr' on it. A stethoscope is a useful signal too. The consultants could have been smartly dressed, both men and women, in business clothing.

If your business employs service engineers who visit either homes or business premises, I believe they should always be in a uniform. This is so inexpensive these days, and can be easily paid for with a slight increase in your call-out charge. This alone will reap untold rewards in confidence and trust from your customers.

Whether you are a self-employed business person or part of a major corporation, your business must have a brand. How you are perceived as an individual will either enhance or detract from that brand. Let's take a simple example. McDonald's is a major worldwide brand, whether you like it or not. All McDonald's staff who interact with customers are dressed in conformance with the brand image. This rule is policed ruthlessly, and quite rightly so. Some small independent fast-food outlets allow their staff to wear whatever clothes suit their fancy. This is not conducive to good hygiene in handling food, and does nothing to build up the brand.

When IBM became the most powerful brand in the office equipment industry, all the staff who had any contact with customers had to wear dark suits with white shirts. I am well aware that in today's business climate there is a tendency for men in the City of London not to wear a tie. This is of course a fashion trend. I have no difficulty with this, as in the majority of cases the remainder of their outfit is smart and fits the image.

So check yourself over. Does your appearance fit the image of your brand? Does it build confidence and trust with your prospective clients and existing customers? An unkempt appearance can easily give the impression of sloppy work. On the other hand, haven't you noticed with your family, close personal friends and colleagues, that when people are experiencing a time of major worry, stress or one of those dips in their lives that we all have from time to time, they take less care of their appearance? They don't bother so much with hair, grooming, or take care or pride in their choice of clothes. (This only applies to those who normally do make an effort: the important indicator here is a change.)

As a counterbalance, wearing your success on your person at work can make clients wary. So it might be prudent to save the big fat 18-carat gold Rolex for playtime. But you must be your own judge of your brand and your marketplace.

In developing the skills and attributes of a people person, a basic understanding of body language is a must. There are some 750,000 body language signals, of which about 15,000 different signals can be identified from facial movements and expressions alone. On an average day the average person communicates with roughly 4,000 verbal sounds. All that is fairly useless information, but it has a purpose in illustrating that although the majority of people are able to control what they say, it is virtually impossible to control all of our body language communicators.

Now the purpose here is not so much to urge you to control your own body language, as to emphasize the importance of being able to read other people's. There are of course occasions when it is necessary to control your own body language. If you are an extrovert you are more likely to touch people or to invade their personal space. Your handshake may be too strong and long. When you realize you are dealing with a more introverted person, at times you may need to give them space. His or her body language can show you this.

As a simple example, when introverts sit down they tend to push their chair slightly back, whereas extroverts will push their chair slightly forward. If you get too close to introverts you will be causing them unnecessary pressure, and they will not relax in your company.

In the imprecise science of body language it is stated that the pupil of the eye will dilate as a sign of approval and constrict for disapproval. A rather amusing experiment was carried out on television to prove the point that people warm to people with enlarged pupils more than they do to those with small pupils. Identical female twins were positioned in front of a studio audience. They were both given drugs. One twin's drug was to make the pupil dilate, and the other's was to make the pupil constrict. A man from the audience was brought forward and asked which of the two girls he would choose. He replied, 'Well, they are both beautiful.' The presenter said, 'That was not my question.' The man selected the girl with the larger pupils.

This again might seem to be fairly useless information, but there is a point to be made. The most important aspect of body language is not what can be described as someone's steady state, but changes from that state. We all know that if people go into bright sunlight their pupils constrict, and if they go into a darkened room they dilate. Now suppose you are in a business meeting and your prospective client is saying she is not sure whether to go ahead with your proposal. If you happen to notice that her pupils are unusually large, that will be one sign from her body language that she feels approval towards you. What she is not saying in words could well be that she wants to go ahead, but hopes to reduce your price.

Whenever body language is in conflict with the spoken word, the body language gives you the correct information. Here are a few more examples that you should be able to use in your day-to-day life. Try never to have a meeting facing the person across a desk. When two people directly face each other, in body language terms this implies conflict. Always try to be seated side by side. Apart from anything else, a table or desk creates a barrier.

If someone is sitting with his arms folded, this could be read as a body language signal that he is not interested in your proposition. However, it could well mean that he is just comfortable sitting that way. Watch for a change. If he had been relaxed, then suddenly folds his arms, it suggests he is switching off. On the other hand if he has been sitting defensively with arms folded, then suddenly unfolds them and leans forward, it could mean he is becoming interested. Have you noticed that people trying to sell something often sit on the edge of a chair and lean forward, and the person being sold to leans right back? It's more productive to leave psychological room for the prospective client to approach you.

Next time you are in a public place, a bar for example, and you notice two people sitting together, observe their body language. If they both have their legs crossed in the direction that angles them towards the other individual, they are very much in tune. If either one has his or her legs crossed and angled away from the other person, then the two are not in tune at that moment. If both individuals have crossed legs angled away from the other person, it can be an indication that they are bored with each other's company and are just going through the motions. Let me reiterate that this is an imprecise science, with many variables, but the clues you gain can still be useful.

One of the most common questions I am asked is how to tell when a person is lying. Again, let me state that with all the research and technological advances that have been made, there is still no absolutely guaranteed way. But for a reader of body language, it is a fairly accurate indicator when you ask someone a question and his or her hand somehow moves involuntarily towards the head and touches the ear, nose or mouth.

This is an indication that what the person just said might not be strictly true. However, a person who is continually touching his or her face might not be lying continually: it could just be a nervous habit. Again, changes in body language are what is important.

According to scientist Professor Albert Mehrabian, body language makes up the most important and largest percentage of the three major components of communication. It far surpasses how you speak and what you say. A staggering 93 per cent of communication relies on aspects other than the words you use.

So watch people's faces. Their expressions can be an indication of what is going through their mind. Changes in expressions need to be watched most carefully.

Some schools of thought encourage sales people to copy the body language of the person they are talking to. I personally do not recommend this practice. When we are communicating with someone, none of us can help subconsciously copying the other person's body language, but a conscious imitation tends to come across as false. Anyone with any real awareness will notice this quickly, and will probably find it smarmy and creepy.

The King's New Clothes is really a fun way of reminding us that other people's perceptions of who and what we are may be very different from our own perceptions. To become a person with whom others like to do business, you must be extremely observant of their facial expressions and body language.

Pocket Reminders

■ Dress to your brand image.
■ Read body language.
■ Make people safe with your style and not threatened.

Wise words

Most people think of changing the world but very few think of changing themselves.

6

Hook the Fish

The toughest challenge for the business winner in the current trading environment is to get a meeting with a decision maker. My fishing friends tell me this is very similar to their biggest challenge – to hook the fish. They say that in order to do so you must have the right bait for the type of fish you want to catch. Those who fly fish can have dozens of different flies, but once they have a fish on the line the fish is invariably landed. Yes of course there is great skill in landing the fish, but the real preparation and effort goes into getting the fish to take the bait. We shall talk more about 'the one that got away' in Chapter 8.

Winning business is no different. Planning and developing a strategy to win new clients is paramount. I am sure you have gathered that this thought process is directed at proactivity: in other words, going out to find new business, in contrast to waiting for the phone to ring or the mail to arrive, which is reactive and passive. I do accept that you are likely to get enquiries either by phone, email or letter. I urge you to respond fast: ideally within an hour of receipt of the enquiry. Demonstrate your efficiency by speed, and best of all respond by telephone. Please also accept that the people who are enquiring of you may also be enquiring of others.

Responding on the telephone will immeasurably increase your chance of success, as it gives you the opportunity to talk and find out exactly what that prospective customer may be needing or looking for. If your product or service does not match the prospect's requirements, as least build your reputation by recommending somewhere else for him or her to go. Remember you are a brand, and every time people touch your brand, endeavour to give them a 'feel-good experience'. Sometimes in conversation it opens the door for you to cross-sell another of your products or services. These enquiries can come from reputation, recommendation, promotional and marketing activity as well as your website.

I do recommend that everyone in business has a website. It is staggering the growth of business that is now done via the internet. Websites should be created with prospective customers in mind. Every business should have the winning culture of 'customer-led and sales driven'. So once again put yourself in the shoes of the customer. When a prospective customer visits your website, he or she will want to see immediately:

■ what you do;
■ what you can do for that person and/or his or her business;
■ that the site is easy to navigate;
■ that the site is regularly updated.

Please endeavour to cut out any time-wasting gimmicks. Speed and usable information easily obtained is the winning formula. (Feel free to check whether I do as I suggest: visit my business's site, www.denny.co.uk. Any comments will be gratefully received and acknowledged.) It is no good having an all-singing and all-dancing website if no one visits it, so it must be promoted. I am not an expert on this subject: we outsource this to people who have this expertise. If you need help, send us an e-mail and we can point you in the right direction.

Before we leave the subject of developing the reactive response, here is a checklist of some other promotional avenues:

- names found in trade directories;
- names found in Yellow Pages or similar;
- advertising (yes, it is worthwhile in some instances);
- leaflet drops;
- inserts in journals and newspapers;
- PR activity.

Of all of the above methods, your most cost-effective publicity can come from PR. During the last recession, when UK unemployment reached 4 million, I produced two audio cassettes, one on how to get a job and one on how to pass an interview. We spent some £5,000 on quarter-page advertisements in selected publications our market research advised us the unemployed would read. These cassettes sold for £5.99 and we sold approximately 100. A biweekly newspaper, *The Executive Post*, reviewed the tapes and gave them a glowing critique. It very kindly included our company details, and we sold in excess of 400 tapes as a result.

This was a valuable lesson. Although the media we advertised in may have been read by many unemployed people, these readers were not prepared to invest in themselves. Perhaps they believed it was the government's responsibility to find them a job. *The Executive Post* was read by executives and professionals, who accepted that it was their responsibility to get themselves back into work. I might add that I lost a great deal of money on the advertisement, but the lesson I learnt has been repaid to me countless times, and that was in itself a good investment. As we all know, we really do learn by our mistakes. The mistake in this case was failing to identify clearly the marketplace and the prospective customers. I should have researched which people would be prepared to invest in themselves, rather than believe that everyone who was unemployed was a potential customer. The lesson taught me you should, first, do your own research and decide on the market for your product, then clearly match the brand to the potential market.

As an example, Aston Martin cars are not advertised in the *Daily Mirror*, because (with the greatest respect to the *Daily Mirror*) its readers are not their target market. Aston Martin has a very clear image of its customer profile, and markets to that profile, using the publications potential customers are most likely to be reading. Another example is Tesco, which has a different customer profile from, say, Waitrose.

Hooking the fish – making an appointment

Stage 1

Now let's go back to the theme of hooking the fish. In this fishing analogy you are not a trawler. Most trawlers do set out with the right nets to scoop up the fish they really want, but let's take it you are a solitary angler with only one line. So the first stage must be to decide on your exact potential customer or client profile. Who do you want to do business with, and who could possibly benefit from your product or service? This probably sounds obvious, but I have to tell you the exercise is very rarely carried out.

If you are in the business to business sector, you can probably compile a list of all your target customers. You need the company name, the decision maker's name, his or her title, the address and telephone number. In compiling this list may I suggest you follow the rule in Figure 6.1.

Too many failing businesses make the costly error of spreading themselves too far and wide. Of course, the target area depends on your type of business. You might decide that

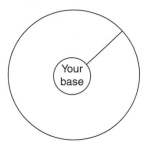

Figure 6.1   Your prospective customers

your radius is only one mile, and that within that mile there is more potential business than you can cope with. Others might have to extend the radius to 20 miles. The failing business that spreads itself over a huge radius wastes too much money travelling. A large target area also makes it virtually impossible to maximize the brand through local PR and promotional activity. People generally much prefer to do business locally rather than further afield.

People running failing businesses might find it an ego trip to claim that they do business internationally and countrywide. True, there are exceptions to the rule (if it is in your customers' interest for you to work across a wide territory), but I certainly wouldn't base my salary or future on the exceptions. Always check on your target audience by asking yourself this simple question: *Is what I am saying or promoting of importance and interest to them?*

In the 1970s I was advising one of the largest franchise companies in the world at that time, Service Master. When it first started in the United States it initially sold huge chunks of territory to single franchisees: for example Chicago, Los Angeles or New York. It quickly discovered that it was impossible for one franchisee to develop the potential, so it had to renegotiate the contracts and split the territories. They kept on splitting. Each time they split, the new franchisees' income was greater than that of the original franchisee who had owned the whole of the territory. Today those great cities probably have 20 franchises. The same has been proved worldwide. Give a franchisee too big a territory and it will never develop its full potential.

In compiling the list it is obvious that you must get the right name of the decision maker. That is the person with the:

■ means or money;
■ authority;
■ need.

Some research has been done to measure the success rate when a sales person has the decision maker in the room at the time of the presentation. On those occasions a 45 per cent success rate was achieved. On the other hand, when the sales person spoke to a replacement for the decision maker (people who said, 'Don't worry, he or she will act upon my recommendation,' or something similar), the success rate was only 8 per cent. Enough said.

So dial the company up and ask the switchboard operator quite simply, 'Can you help me, please? (Pause and wait for the reply.) 'Who is responsible for...?' Once you have got the name, make sure you have the first name and surname and how the person prefers to be addressed. Finally, do a double-check. 'So am I right in thinking that Mr X is responsible for purchasing...?' You will find that on some occasions the receptionist answers, 'Oh no, Ms Z handles that.' Once you have the name, do not ask to be connected immediately. If you are asked why you want the name, you can say that you want to make sure your letter is addressed correctly to the right person, or (only a slight fib) that you have been asked to send some information and you want to make sure it gets to the right person.

If you have difficulties it is also possible to go to a company's website and get the information that way.

Just as a guideline, I recommend that every business winner should have a prospect database of 50 prospects he or she is hoping or wanting to do business with. This database must be topped up continually.

Stage 2

You must now decide whether to make your first approach by telephone or by letter. I recommend a letter, but there are occasions when a telephone call is highly suitable.

The letter
The purpose of an initial letter (such as in Figure 6.2, 6.3 or 6.4) is to sell your follow-up telephone call, which in turn should sell an appointment for a face-to-face meeting. When you send your letter, I recommend that you do not include brochures or product literature. You can leave these till after your meeting. I accept that if your business is direct to consumer, this advice will not be appropriate to you. If you are in that category, there are occasions when it is more suitable to market passively. You may wish to send a brochure or leaflet directly to your database of prospects.

When you are creating such a brochure or leaflet it must clearly shout out the benefits you can provide to customers. May I remind you, you are not focusing on your business, product or service. You should be stating what it will do for your prospective customers, and there is a big difference here.

At my live business training seminars I ask the delegates during the coffee breaks to introduce themselves to each other, and ask the people they talk to what their business is. I stress the importance of giving the benefit of your business first. In other words, explain the results of your product or service. At

Mr J Smith
Job Title
Company Name
Address

Dear Mr Smith

May I introduce myself and my company/firm to you?

The purpose of this letter is to inform you that we have one or two new developments within our product/ service/range that may be of interest to you.

I obviously have no idea at this stage whether this is the case, so I shall be telephoning you within the next two or three days to see if we may be able to fix up a very short meeting where I can explain in more detail.

I really look forward to speaking to you.

Yours sincerely

(Signature)

Name (typed)
Job title

Figure 6.2   Sample letter to a B to B prospect

Mr J Smith
Job Title
Company Name
Address

Dear Mr Smith

The purpose of writing to you is to introduce myself and my company.

We specialize in .... and I believe some of our products/ services could well be of interest. I also believe that they might save/make you a great deal of money.

I obviously have no idea whether this may be of interest, so I shall give you a call within the next two or three days to see if we can arrange a very short meeting.

Yours sincerely

(Signature)

Name (typed)

Figure 6.3 Sample letter to a B to B prospect

Joe Bloggs
Joe Bloggs Associates
24 Market Way
Chipsdean
Westmanshire
CH2 8BL

Dear Joe

You may have heard that .... are now delivering 'THE best value for money .... services in the UK' – not our quote, but one from our customers.

The purpose of this letter is to see whether we can arrange a very short meeting for you to see whether what we are currently able to achieve may be of interest to Joe Bloggs Associates, now or in the future.

I shall phone you in the next two to three days to see when we could have a 20–25 minutes get-together.

Yours sincerely

(Signature)

Name (typed)
Job title

PS In most cases we can guarantee to reduce costs, improve service and simplify administration.

Figure 6.4 Sample letter to a B to B prospect

one event I went up to a delegate and said, 'And what do you do?' He hesitated for a minute, then said, 'We make people feel comfortable in their homes.' I replied, 'Oh, that's interesting. How do you do that?' He said, 'We manufacture chairs.' The moral of the story is that we are all interested in the results of a product or service, but not necessarily so interested in just the product or service.

Let me give you another example. You might meet someone at a social function, introduce yourself and then ask what that person does for a living. If she says, 'I sell life insurance,' you might well be tempted to find someone else to talk to. But if she replies, 'I care for people at times of great tragedy or great loss,' you might well respond, 'Oh really! How do you do that?'

Far too many brochures and leaflets are a complete waste of money. They can be an ego trip for the business. Your brochure or literature must be an attention getter within two to three seconds. It must motivate the recipient to find out more. So make it easy for recipients to contact you by telephone, email and so on, and then respond fast.

The telephone call

This is probably the activity that many people dislike and dread more than any other. In all honesty the only reason it is disliked is that there is a fear of rejection. The other person might say, 'I'm too busy,' or 'No, I'm not interested.' And quite frankly this isn't really all that bad.

So here is the process. Dial up the company, and when the switchboard answers, this is what you say:

John Smith, please.

The operator will almost certainly say:

Who's calling?

Your response should be:

> Richard Denny. (Only say this if your name is in fact Richard Denny. Hic!)

Never use a title such as Mr, Miss, Mrs or Ms. Also please don't waste time with the operator by saying 'Would you put me through to Mr Smith, please?' or even worse, 'Can I speak to Mr Smith, please?'

Very few telephonists, receptionists or operators are properly trained, so their next response to you is likely to be:

> From where?

Personally I reply:

> From Moreton-in-Marsh (the location of my head office).

This elicits a deathly hush on the other end of the phone, and I get put through. The operator now hasn't a clue. Is this a place? Is this a company? Because the receptionist is dumbfounded, he or she wants to get rid of you as quickly as possible, and puts you through. He or she just won't know how to handle that reply.

If you are asked the name of your company, give it. If you are asked why you are calling, say it is in connection with your correspondence.

If for any reason your contact is not available, always say that you will call back, and ask for the most convenient time.

Now let's proceed with the conversation to secure the appointment:

> Hello, Mr Smith. This is Richard Denny here of the Richard Denny Group. Is it convenient to speak for a couple of minutes?

(you get a reply)

Did you get my letter? The purpose of my ringing you, as I said in my letter, is that we have one or two products/services that may be of great interest to you. But I really have no idea at this stage, and in order to save a great deal of time may I suggest that we arrange a short meeting at your convenience? I don't know if you have a diary available, but would 9.20 next Thursday be convenient? Or some time the following week?

Let's now analyse this very basic telephone procedure. Please bear in mind that you must adapt this outline to suit your own personality and industry.

- Do not attempt to sell or discuss your products in detail on the telephone. If they can be sold on the phone, why do you want an appointment? If you must talk about your products or services, only talk about the results. But best of all, leave this area alone.
- Do not make a statement that you cannot justify.
- Do not offer an appointment on the hour, as it appears as if you could be there for one hour.
- Do not offer an appointment on the half hour, as this implies a half-hour meeting.
- Always choose an unusual time, as this implies that the meeting will be short. I shall repeat it once again: a decision maker's time is precious. So why would he or she want to meet a complete stranger and give that person one hour out of his or her own bank account of time?
- If your prospect says 'Can't you put something in the post?' the common sense approach is of course to say, 'The purpose of my wishing to see you is that I can leave you with just the information you would be really interested in. Apart from that, Mr Smith, I would really like to meet you.'

Let me tell you a short story. On one of my courses I was asked by a health and safety executive (who was endeavouring to sell health and safety!) why he was having such difficulty in getting appointments. I asked him what he said, and he replied, 'I do everything you described in identifying decision makers, and I phone them. I ask them if I can come to talk to them about health and safety.' As you can imagine, his most common reply was, 'I'm extremely busy at the moment.' He was getting massive resistance. I suggested that he try the following phraseology (adapted to suit his own personality): 'Mr/Ms X, may I come and discuss with you how my organization can save you a great deal of money, time and worry in preventing health and safety claims?'

The above example illustrates the point that so few people in business are actively doing it right. Think and talk about the benefits to your prospective client or customer.

Voicemail

We are all experiencing an increased use of voicemail. When you are following up a letter and are confronted with voicemail, you have two choices: either leave a message or phone again. My preference and advice is to call again. It is pretty useless to ask your recipient to return your call. In my experience only the very best business people return calls. It appears that weak and poorly organized individuals do not. My final suggestion is to try phoning outside normal business hours, or get the mobile telephone number of your contact from the switchboard or secretary.

This can be difficult, so here is a little tip. When asking for a mobile number try this phraseology:

Can you help me please? (Pause and wait for the reply.) I promised Mr Smith I would call him. We seem to be missing each other. Have you got a mobile number that I can make contact with him on?

Some tips on making excellent telephone calls

■ Always smile while you are speaking on the telephone. It does project a better telephone manner.
■ Be enthusiastic. Enthusiasm is very infectious.
■ Always plan your call before you pick up the phone.
■ Decide exactly what you want to achieve before you dial.
■ Have the courtesy to put yourself in the other person's shoes.

This chapter is all about proactivity – your life and success in your hands. That is the place it should be, and the place where it is safest of all. Here are a few more tips to work on. Research has shown that firms that dominate the market:

■ are 60 per cent more likely to have sales goals;
■ are twice as likely to use business development specialists;
■ are 30 per cent more likely to proactively seek referrals;
■ secure one-third more clients through strategic partners;
■ are three times more likely to have formal agreements with referral partners.

Hooking the fish is a challenge and requires thought, planning and the selection of the appropriate bait, as the successful fisher would agree. And the right bait is phraseology that will attract your potential customer. The ideas I am giving you work, and have been tried and tested literally hundreds of thousands of times.

Pocket Reminders

■ Decide on your customer profile.
■ Don't spread yourself too thinly.
■ Build a prospect list.
■ Be proactive.
■ Plan your calls and meetings.
■ Use the right bait to attract the right fish.

Wise words

A negative attitude cancels out positive skills.

7

The First Meeting

From now on the process of winning business is much more enjoyable. It is very debilitating for a business winner to have a blank diary with no new appointments, so prevent the stress and have some meetings to look forward to. There are basically two types of first meeting, and I shall deal with each one separately.

The first is the reactive enquiry: in other words, an email, telephone or letter asking what you do/can do, or requesting a price. If the enquiry warrants it, you will no doubt arrange a time and date to meet. This could be on your premises or the prospect's. It is always worthwhile (if the potential warrants it) to have a meeting. This can be arranged with the following type of phraseology:

> Let's meet up. It'll save a lot of time. Then I can be absolutely sure of your specific requirements, which will enable me to give you the very best possible help and price.

Your percentage chance of success is always much higher when your prospect comes to you. It really shows his or her commitment. However this cannot always be arranged. I might add that on the back of an enquiry you really should be looking to have a minimum 60 to 70 per cent success rate on winning new business.

If you are not currently experiencing this success rate, it could be that your promotional activity is not in line with your prospective customer profile. In other words, you are pitching your brand and service to the wrong audience. Alternatively, you might find that you have a really poor and weak first meeting. The detail of that will unfold in this chapter. If this meeting results in your being asked to prepare a proposal, do it fast. To remove any misunderstanding, fast means within hours (days, or a maximum of one week). How to deliver this proposal is revealed later in the book.

The second type of first meeting is what I shall refer to as the introductory meeting. This is a meeting fixed on the back of the proactive approach outlined in the last chapter. You are going to meet a possible source of new business at his or her premises. As with almost everything that leads to success in life, a little bit of planning and preparation is essential. What do you know about the customer? Have you done a little research, from the company website or another of the numerous sources of information available?

It might even be helpful if you can find out who the business's current suppliers are. In this instance, the more you know about your competitors' products and/or services, and their strengths and weaknesses, the more it will undoubtedly help you. Let me put in a proviso here. It is a golden rule of business winners never to directly criticize a competitor. Instead you can use your knowledge of its weaknesses to help you promote your strengths, when you get into that sort of detail.

Let's create a typical scenario of a business to business (B2B) opportunity. You arrive at the premises and no doubt will be greeted by a receptionist and told to take a seat. Under no circumstances whatsoever should you sit down in reception. Let me briefly explain. You arrive feeling positive, with enthusiasm and a little adrenalin running. You are told to take a seat, and if you do, you will find that most reception chairs are fairly low. Other people will pass through the reception, and the situation means you will feel subservient as they look down at you. (In body language, height creates a feeling of superiority.) Subconsciously your enthusiasm will diminish. People on horseback are often regarded as toffee-nosed because they look down at people in their cars or on foot. If you stand, you will indicate to others – including the receptionist – that you are an important person. You will also be at the same height if your prospect comes to get you for the meeting.

Now let's put you in the other person's shoes. He or she has a meeting arranged with you, but is more than likely a little unsure why you want it, and no doubt a little suspicious as well. Possibly the person is concerned that you might try to sell him or her something the organization does not want or need. He or she might also be wondering what you are like as a person, and will almost certainly be concerned that you might take up too much of his or her time.

Let's continue with our scenario. You now go into the person's office and sit down. The normal exchange of polite greetings, mention of the weather, the journey and parking, takes place. This should be kept short and sweet – 5 to 10 seconds. Hand over your business card and commence your meeting with something like this:

Well, it's really good to meet you.

I am going to endeavour to use your time constructively.

May I suggest that I briefly tell you a little about me and my firm/company/business, then if I may, find out a little bit about what you do. If at the end of our short discussion there is interest from your side in some of the things we do, perhaps we could arrange another get-together.

From my perspective it goes without saying that the reason I have arranged this meeting is that we would really like to do some business with you and your firm/company/business.

It is far better to make this sort of statement than go through some charade or pretence. Your prospect obviously knows why you are there, so why pretend otherwise? I personally get frustrated with people who come to see me, then waffle on and can't get to the point.

Now explain in a few sentences what you do. Start by stating the results of your product and/or service, then give a little more detail of what you do and how. You can also drop in here one or two of your other clients' names, if this would be an endorsement of your credibility. But please do not dwell too much on that: just the company name will suffice. This section of the first meeting should take no longer than two to three minutes, unless of course your prospect wants more information, detail or clarification.

Now comes the main purpose of your being there. That is for you to assess whether you want to do business with this prospect, and to find out what areas of product or service you supply could match the company's requirements, *needs and wants*. There is such a big difference between a need and a want. The rule of thumb is that people will always find the money and/or will to do what they want, but won't necessarily find it for what they need.

Let me give you a very simple example. A man in his thirties, married with two children, will more than likely spend £20 a month on beer or wine, but might well not have any life insurance. The role of the life insurance business winner is to turn that need into a want.

So let's continue with the scenario. This is the most important communication and selling skill of all time, and will be forever. I am asked countless thousands of times, what is the greatest skill learnt and then demonstrated by the most successful and wealthy super sales people in the world? My reply is always the same. It is the skill of *asking the right questions*. Now I cannot tell you exactly what questions you should be asking, because every product and service requires different information gathering.

Let me tell you a short story. I wanted a laptop computer, and I arranged for three different suppliers to send in an expert. The first arrived with a laptop, and proceeded to give me an excellent demonstration explaining all the features and benefits. He then endeavoured to persuade me to buy it. I politely got rid of him by saying that I wished to think about it. The second individual arrived, again with his brand of laptop. This was also a thoroughly professional and knowledgeable presentation, including details on the guarantee, service contract and instruction booklet. I politely did the same as before, with a 'Thank you very much and I'll think about it.' The third expert arrived without anything other than a paper notebook. He went through the pleasantries, then proceeded to ask me why I wanted a laptop. I recall my initial reply, which was, 'Well, everybody else seems to have one.' He expertly refrained from falling off his chair in mirth, and kept his head down, taking notes. His next question was, if I did have one, what would I initially like to use it for? He then proceeded with a string of very constructive questions which opened up my mind to the possibilities in using a laptop. In the process he inspired the emotional feeling of 'I really want.' After about 10 or 15 minutes of discussion he then said, 'I think I have got exactly what you are looking for.' He went out to his car and brought me a laptop (almost certainly the only one he had with him). He then proceeded to explain how his laptop would do what I was looking for. You can guess who got the order.

Winning new business really is so easy. I am just amazed why so many people make a complete pig's ear of it.

Let's revert to our scenario. You are with your prospect on your first meeting. Let me ask you, what did you hope to achieve from this meeting? If your expectation was that you would leave with a new piece of business, you were in cloud cuckoo land. Now am not saying that this isn't possible, because of course it is. You might have arrived at just the right time. Perhaps your prospect had been let down by a previous supplier. Perhaps changes in circumstances meant the firm now suddenly needed or wanted what you had to offer – in which case this is good luck. I might add that being lucky only happens to those who are positive and proactive. Certainly no one ever becomes lucky without some degree of doing. Every single successful person will always claim that some of his or her success has come from luck. People who do not achieve to their potential always seem to state that they have been unlucky, or are just not lucky.

Now check yourself. Are you one of those who make things happen, those who watch things happen, or those who wonder what happened? Whichever category you are in, now it is in your power and control to change if you so wish.

Realistically your objective should be to leave the meeting with a date for another meeting, or at least for the other person to feel you are a really nice person. The prospect should have enjoyed the meeting and felt it was not a waste of his or her time. In other words you have started the foundation of a new relationship. There might even be a recommendation from the person at some future stage. I know I am being repetitive, but business is all about people and relationships. Everyone you meet could become your ambassador, and an ambassador of your brand, so just bear that in mind.

Let's get back to the first meeting, and the issue of asking questions. These can always be prefaced with how, what, why, when or where. As well as gathering information that will enable you to discuss relevant products and services for your prospect, you must not lose sight of the end objective – which is to sell yourself. The way to achieve that, as I have already stated, is to show genuine interest in the other person. So don't be afraid to ask questions that may appear to be slightly personal. For example, 'How long have you been here? What were you doing before? How did you get into this industry? What are your biggest challenges? What currently are your biggest worries?'

As we all know, a really good conversation is not one-sided, and in developing your skills to be a real people person it is therefore necessary to develop your listening skills. The better you listen and respond to others, the better they will listen and respond to you. The more attention you pay when someone else is talking, the more attention he or she will pay to you when you are talking. This is best described as active listening. Think of listening based on the ratio of having two ears and one mouth. It is great for your business if you can develop the skill of listening twice as much as you speak. It will help you to do this if you maintain eye contact. It shows that you are paying attention. Concentrate, do not let yourself be thinking of the next question or a response to the reply. Listen to what is being said. It is not unacceptable for you to think about why the person is saying that.

In a business meeting it is quite acceptable to make notes. This will reinforce your memory. Sometimes it is advisable to seek permission first. This is very rarely refused. I do not recommend people to use a recording device, unless they are journalists, in which case I thoroughly recommend it. Allow people to finish their sentences, and always pause before replying. Pausing will add power to what you say, and it also indicates that you are giving a considered response. Some people with enthusiasm tend to talk too quickly, and there are others of course who speak far too slowly. Just get the balance right, and be aware of your own failings and determined to correct them.

All the time during this first meeting, keep stepping into the other person's shoes, then step out again and consider what you say. Watch the person's facial expressions and body language as well as listening to what he or she is saying.

No doubt if you have selected your prospective client/customer correctly and he or she has 'bought' you as a person, he or she will also be interested in your products and services. It is so important at this first meeting that your prospect understands the results and the successes that you have achieved for other clients. If the nature of your business is such that you cannot disclose names, no matter, but do offer one or two case histories, stories or examples. These must be relevant to the prospect's interests or industry. I make all of these points even though they are common sense, because far too many who have not been trained in the skills of selling continually make the mistake of doing the opposite to what I have just stated.

Nobody really wants to hear how clever or brilliant you have been on something that is totally irrelevant to their own situation. Far from being a positive it is a big switch-off.

Also be careful when asking more personal questions that you don't become too familiar. I personally will always ask whether I can use a person's first name before doing so, but I always insist right from the outset that the other person calls me Richard.

Here is another little thought worth bearing in mind at these first meetings. That is to wear the hat of a solution provider rather than a problem giver. Let me illustrate what I mean. We recently required some refurbishment to our bathrooms. Three of the four plumbing contractors who were invited to quote for the work sucked air through their teeth, shook their heads and gave my wife Dorothy and me more problems than we had ever envisaged. One plumber looked at every problem as an opportunity, and only talked about solutions, offering alterna- tives. Even though he was quite a bit more expensive than the others, he got the contract. Isn't it amazing how we all make decisions? Very rarely are they based entirely on logic.

I want now to generalize about two types of people. The first is the individual who is a little shy, inclined to be introverted, and possibly dreads meetings with complete strangers. If you are this sort of person, let me reassure you. In all my 40-odd years of business, which have included more meetings than I could possibly count, I have to say that on only two occasions have I met a person whom I found to be unpleasant, rude and offensive. On those occasions the meeting lasted about five minutes, and it ended at my instigation, with a comment like, 'Well, you are obviously very busy. You call me when you are ready to increase your profits, make more money, be more successful and less stressed. Now is obviously not the right time. Goodbye.' On every other occasion I have found people to be friendly, kind, considerate and pleasant to meet. However, I also have to say that not every meeting has resulted in business.

So just look forward to your meetings, in the frame of mind that you are going to meet a really nice person. This will help your own mindset.

Now let's go to the other extreme. This is the person who thinks he or she is a bit of a character, and no doubt has a high opinion of him/herself and an ego to match. This individual sadly will not be buying this book, but may well be given it! If you are a big enough person to have got this far, good on you. All I can say is that subconsciously you will have changed to become more of a people person whom others would like to do business with. The only risk here is that people like this can be such know-all smarty pants that they convince themselves there is no need for them to develop personally, and there is nothing new in the advice I am giving. Let me just challenge those individuals. How much new business are you bringing in?

We are now coming to the conclusion to the successful first meeting, to which there are really only five possible outcomes.

■ First, you decide there really is no opportunity for you to do business. Either your product or service doesn't match the customer's needs, or the customer has requirements that you cannot possibly meet. In that case, the sooner you wrap the meeting up the better, so you do not waste any more of each other's time. You could use this situation, however, as an opportunity to obtain a referral. Try a phrase such as this. 'Thank you so much for seeing me. I really do appreciate it, but there is obviously nothing we can do together. But if we reversed roles and you were sitting where I am sitting, who do you think I should be talking to?'

■ The polite 'No.' In other words, the person is not going to change from the current supplier and is in no position to do business with you today. I want to stress now that this is a big opportunity for the future, and not to be dismissed lightly. I cover this situation in the next chapter.

■ The prospective client indicates that he or she would like to arrange another meeting for you with others in the organization. This is of course is a very positive outcome, and you must endeavour before leaving to arrange a date and time. Use this sort of phraseology. 'OK, that's a really good idea. As we all know people's diaries are a bit of a nightmare, so let's see whether we can do it now. We both have our diaries and that's at least a start.'

■ Fourth, your prospective client wants to fix up a more detailed meeting with you personally. This again is a really positive result. As before, don't leave without fixing up a date and time. Use words to the effect of, 'Great. I've got my diary with me, so let's save some time by fixing a date now.' This proactivity will make it clear whether the offer is genuine, or you have been talking to a weak prospect who is saying 'Let's meet again' but in reality has no intention of doing so.

■ Finally, there is the rare and *lucky* occasion when the prospective client would like to be sent a proposal, quotation or estimate. Endeavour to control your enthusiasm until you are outside the building. Realistically, you must again take control, so the next stage in this scenario is for you to go away and prepare a document, quote, proposal or estimate. Now we come to another golden rule. Break this at your peril. For business you really want to win, do not post, email or fax the document. You must take it in and hand it over personally.

Here again, say something like this, but change the phraseology to suit your personality. 'Thank you, Mr/Ms X. Today is Wednesday. We'll work on this immediately, and can get back to you by Monday of next week. Which would be more suitable for me to bring it, Monday or Tuesday, morning or afternoon? What time would suit you best?' If he or she replies, 'Oh no, there's no need for another meeting. Just email it or post it,' you should respond with, 'It will save a lot of your time if I bring it. We can go through it, and you can tell me whether it's what you were hoping for.'

Let me give you another personal example. We needed an architect to do some work on our home. We selected three architects, each of whom visited and took the details. In due course we had the first response, which consisted of an outline proposal and a covering letter. The final line was, 'If I can be of any further service please do not hesitate to contact me.' As you can imagine, what did I look for first? The price, of course. The proposer endeavoured to hide it, but I found it. I then received the second missive, which was almost identical to the first, with the same last line. The third architect phoned me and said that he had prepared some ideas, and could he come to see us. I replied, 'Of course.' He then asked when my wife would be available (he knew who the boss was), and we fixed up a meeting. I might add that when we met I was aware his services were a long way short of being the cheapest, and his concepts weren't necessarily the best. But he gave us great confidence in his ability with our project, and he got the job. The other two architects never even followed us up, and we wonder to this day whether they are still in business.

The theme here is, never give the next move to your client or customer, and do not ever put yourself in an old-fashioned, hard-selling, pushy situation.

You should be able to see that it is a bad tactic to finish a letter by suggesting the other person should contact you. We all know that invariably he or she won't. The result is that you have to keep chasing him or her, and that is being pushy. If on rare occasions you do have to send your proposal by letter, email or fax, always sign off with this sort of thing. 'I hope that the enclosed is what you are expecting. I shall give you a call in the next 24 hours to make sure that you received it, and to make sure that it is what you were hoping for.' By being proactive you stay in control. When you meet or speak it gives you the opportunity to ask:

Are you happy with this?

Is this OK?

Always remember to end with, 'I will call you.'

These are decent and respectful questions for you to use to close some business.

Let me recap. There are five possible outcomes of that first meeting. Four of them are really positive, and only one is entirely negative. That's not a bad ratio for potential success.

Pocket Reminders

▓ Respond fast to a reactive enquiry.
▓ Be upfront about why you are there.
▓ There is a big difference between a need and a want.
▓ Become lucky by doing.
▓ A good conversationalist uses two ears and one mouth.
▓ Step in and out of the other person's shoes.
▓ Short meetings with a decision are best of all.

Wise words

Having something to say is always more important than wanting to say something.

8

Go for a 'No'

The title of this chapter may sound ridiculous, and must raise an element of scepticism in you. We all know we don't really want a 'no', we want a 'yes' from a prospective new client. But there are many ways to catch a fish. From our earliest childhood most of us were brought up to understand that a no really means 'no', and we were educated to behave and respond accordingly. But in the world of business a no is really a 'No, not today.'

Early in the book I explained that I despise and abhor pushy hard-selling tactics, but equally I dislike weak wishy-washy behaviour. In business when someone says 'no' it very rarely means 'No, I will never do business with you.' What that person is really saying is, 'No thank you at this moment in time.' Politicians have learnt to never say 'never.'

Let me tell you a couple of stories to illustrate the point.

One part of our business produces training material on DVDs and videos. Back in the 1990s when video training was at its height, one of our people called on the National Westminster Bank's training centre in Heythrop, Gloucestershire, with the intention of first winning a new client, and second, selling some of our video training programmes. The staff politely declined as they didn't have a use for us then, and we got the proverbial 'no'. But we wanted to win this major client. So every three months we popped in to have a chat and show some new productions. This went on for two years. As with all big organizations, the training directors moved on to other responsibilities and new people came in, and we had to start the relationship all over again. Another year went by, then on one of the visits they decided to purchase a few of our productions. The initial order was very small, only about £2,000. Then the orders started to flow. The following year we received our biggest order to date from NatWest, which was slightly in excess of £250,000. The original 'no' was really a 'No, not today'. We wanted the client and were determined to stay with it.

We have all got to accept that we live in a time of dramatic change. Even as individuals in our private lives, our circumstances are continually changing. Statistically it is said more change has taken place in the last 40 years than in the whole history of humankind. I will guarantee that every one of the readers of this book has bought something or done something in the last six months that previously they had said no to. Possibly that was because they did not want or need it. Maybe the time was not right, or perhaps they could not have afforded it. Nevertheless, six months down the line circumstances changed. This is a mindset that all business winners must understand and use to their advantage.

My second story took place in 2005. We were invited to put up a proposal and costings for a project for a major European lift manufacturer. It needed to implement a change programme for all of its staff , from senior management right through to the shop floor. We knew we were up against three other possible providers. In due course my senior management team and I duly made a presentation to the board. We believed we had made an excellent presentation and provided the solutions to the challenges. A week after the presentation we were told we had not won the contract. Naturally we were upset and a little despondent. The following week I wrote a letter to the CEO, which basically said, 'Thank you so much for the chance for us to pitch for the training programme. We were sorry not to have won it, but as far as I am concerned we value relationships. I really value the relationship I have with you, and also the relationships my people built with yours in doing our research. As far as I am concerned the door is not closed, and is always open for whenever we may be able to help you and your company in the future.'

We maintained contact with that client, sending its staff little news items, for about 8 to 10 months. We were then approached to give the company some advice on its sales organization, and how it could be reorganized to develop a customer-led and sales-driven business. It wasn't a huge contract, but nevertheless it resulted in about £30,000 worth of business, which we duly delivered and the company was delighted. I use this as a second example to illustrate to you the importance of valuing relationships in order to be a business winner.

Let's be ridiculous for a few minutes. Imagine a world where the word 'no' did not exist. Just suppose that no one could ever say no to you. Here is the challenge. What would you be doing more of every day? We are going to keep this strictly on a business basis! So in all honesty (and do be honest with yourself here), what would you be doing? I suspect that you would be picking up the phone more often to arrange to see people. You would send out more letters. You would be making quadruple the amount of contacts to offer your services or products.

In this ridiculous example I am trying to point out that the real inhibitor to proactivity is the fear of a prospect saying no. And frankly this is quite possibly the worst thing that can happen to any of us – except that it's not that bad. Realistically a 'no' is only a 'No, not today,' as I have just indicated.

If I was buying a company, I would complete the necessary due diligence and in the process I would uncover details of the turnover, profit, number of employees, and ideally the number of customers, customer spend and customer profile. I would also want to look at the list of 'no, not todays'. I can almost guarantee that very few businesses have this data. From my perspective this is an extremely valuable asset. In our small group of companies our most valuable asset is our people. Our second most valuable asset is our existing client base, and our third is our 'no, not today' list.

If I look to see where our revenue comes from, our biggest source is existing clients. The second biggest business stream comes from people who were on our 'no, not today' list and have been converted into customers. Our third biggest source comes from completely new clients. I know that if we wanted to compete with any business, if my people could only acquire its 'no, not today' prospect list we could make a fortune.

So now that I have (I hope) convinced you of the value of a 'no, not today' opportunity, how can you use this knowledge? I am endeavouring throughout this book to stick to one of our major principles as a skill development company, which is always to provide practical, sensible, realistic and usable ideas that work. I don't work or live in a world of theory. In the business world we should not be theorists but practitioners. So please forgive me if I am being too basic.

Now imagine a business meeting and the conclusion. Your prospect has given you the polite no. This can be voiced in lots of different ways, but it is nonetheless an emphatic no. Here is a simple phraseology for you to adapt:

> Mr/Ms X, it was really good to meet you. I quite understand that there is nothing we can do together at moment. But may I stay in contact? (pause) We are developing our products and services continuously. We never know what is around the corner. Your circumstances may change. Someone might even let you down. So may I stay in contact?

Then pause. You will find 99 times out of 100 that your prospect will say, 'Yes, by all means.' You can then say, 'May I call you again in three to four months? In the meantime we will keep you updated of any new developments. Is that OK?'

You can if you would like say, 'Mr/Ms X, in the meantime if ever you should need or require any of the services or products we supply, please give me a call.'

There is also the situation where you get a no on the follow-up call to your letter asking for an appointment. Your contact says he or she does not want to see you, there is no purpose in your having a meeting, or words to that effect. You could always finish that call by saying:

> OK, I quite understand. But may I keep in contact? We are always developing our services and/or products and you never know, there might be something that is of interest in the future.

Again, pause. In my experience the person will say, 'Yes, by all means.' You then say, 'May I give you a call in three to four months?' (pause) 'In the meantime I will keep you posted with anything that may be of interest. It was nice to speak to you, Mr/Ms X. Goodbye.'

So that is the first stage of turning the 'no' into a 'no, not today.' Now let's move to the second stage and just gently stay in contact. Maybe once a month you send out a newsletter if you have one, or a case history that might be of interest. Perhaps you can send a small giveaway, or a new product brochure. Most important of all are copies of press cuttings.

I was taught by Brian McLaurin of McLaurin Communications, one of the giants in the PR industry, that the real value of PR is not just in getting your story in newspapers, journals, trade magazines and so on, but in what you do with the stories. He said that every time you have some positive news in the media, you should then copy the article and send it to all your clients and prospects. Enclose a compliments slip and preferably a handwritten note saying something like, 'I thought you might be interested in this.' And always sign the slip personally.

In Chapter 11 I cover in even more detail some more ideas where you can demonstrate to your 'no, not todays' that you care. This takes minutes of your time and can make a world of difference in increasing your chances of winning new business. More than likely you will only have between 10 and 20 'no, not todays' that you are in contact with at any given time.

If you follow exactly the procedure and principle of what a 'no, not today' really is, you are going to experience a fundamental change, from dealing with a negative to a positive. Let me remind you once again that your brain works so much better with positive thoughts than with negative thoughts. It is your job and nobody else's to manage your greatest asset. We all have a tendency to put ourselves under too much pressure.

If you strive to get a yes and in the process you get a no, your brain reads this as a failure experience. Do not let your brain have failure experiences unnecessarily. If you feel you have achieved a 'no, not today', this from now on becomes a success experience.

At the height of the economic boom when we were selling our video training programmes, we employed a telesales team. This was a proactive team who were cold-calling prospects with the objective of sending out our trailer videos free of charge on a one-week trial. The team would then follow up with a sales call to win the business. Now as we all know, cold-calling can be a very debilitating occupation. Any cold-calling centre will experience a high churn of staff. The secret of managing such a team is to keep them motivated. Each person was targeted to make a minimum of approximately 80 calls a day, and speak to 15 contacts. Now again, as I am sure you are aware, you get many more nos than yeses, and after a little while the daily call rate per person falls, and there is more time spent on tea breaks, going to the loo, form-filling and any excuse not to pick up the phone. So every so often we would run a competition. We would get the team together in the morning and announce that today we would be competing to see who could get the most nos in a day. Every time people got a no, they would put a tick beside their name on the sales board in the office. The winner got two bottles of wine, the second got a bottle of wine and the third got a box of chocolates. Everybody hit the phones with enthusiasm, and the call rate rocketed. And would you believe it, so did the sales! The team always earned a lot more money in commission on achieving a sale than they did from heading the 'nos' board. There is a powerful message, and a principle for all who want to win business. If you want some yeses you must expect more nos. Statistically it appears that if you have a good product or service and you know what you are doing in the field of communications, the more nos you get, you will also achieve more yeses.

My experience, for what it is worth, has given me a detestation of the phrase, 'I want to think about it.' This is really a polite British way of saying 'not on your Nelly', or words to that effect. This is because most people don't like to offend or give bad news, and generally do not like to upset the other person. On hearing 'I want to think about it' we go away hoping the person really is going to think about it. I am sure you would not base your future on the hopes of a lottery win, so don't lay any hope on a 'think about it'. It is far better to get a straight 'no'.

If I was to sit down with every one of my readers who really do want to increase their business, one of my questions would be, how many nos are you getting? If you aren't getting very many, more than likely you are not being sufficiently proactive.

So never again be fearful of a no. From now on for the rest of your career, a 'no' is only a 'No, not today.'

Pocket Reminders

- Be happy with a no.
- No is only a 'No, not today'.
- Build a 'no, not today' list.
- Despise 'I will think about it'.
- Keep in contact with your 'no' list. There is gold there.

Wise words

If you want to increase your successes, double your failure rate.

9

Present to Win

In *Postive Management: How to Build a Winning Team*, a book published in 1994 which was based upon a study of 62 companies, it was discovered that making a winning presentation was the number one most important factor in securing business. This may seem blatantly obvious. But as is the case with many consultancy contracts, the clients know the answers and all the consultant does is draw out the information and tell them what they already know. The consultant then charges a whacking great fee, especially if the organization is in the public sector. This now gives the executives the moral courage to make a decision, with their arse nicely covered, and for which they will not be held accountable.

This is in no way a criticism of this excellent book and the results of the study, it just highlights the point that common sense is all too uncommon.

Making a winning presentation is of course crucial to winning a bid. Obviously the people to whom the presentation is being made must make a decision, and that can really only be based on what is presented. The objective of the presentation is to convince those listening that this is the team they should place their business with. Now if you intend to be truly professional and convincing, the work carried out prior to the presentation will of course create a match with what the prospective client wants to hear.

For example, have you found out the buying criteria? How will the decision be made? Is it made on price? Will the prospects be looking to go with the cheapest bidder? Are they looking for creativity? Will the decision be based on delivery times? What exactly do they really want? The time spent in researching and asking the right questions to the right people is paramount to presenting the winning bid. There's an old cliché, 'Let's sell them what they really want' – and here we are back to the activity of the majority of consultants.

There are a variety of ways of making presentations, but the majority of the principles are exactly the same, so I shall keep it simple. First of all let's cover the most common type of presentation, which is one to one. In this scenario let's continue with the advice given in Chapter 7. You'll recall, at this point you have had the first meeting with a prospective client, and it has ended with an invitation to you to go away and prepare a proposal, then come back to present it.

Before we go through the presentation itself, let's cover some worthwhile tips about the proposal document. You need to make sure, first, that the document will give you the best possible chance to win the business, and second, that it becomes a good basis for the live face-to-face presentation. It is quite extraordinary how few people who need to prepare estimates, quotations or proposals have ever had any formal training on this extremely important activity. Of course it is then no wonder that so many are full of garbage, are boring, uninteresting, and appear to have been written by the sales prevention department. Let me ask you, what do you want to see in an estimate, quotation or proposal? I would be amazed if your first answer was anything other than price.

Let me again be repetitive. Our marketplace is all about people. You are not hoping to win business from a company, firm, organization, house or factory, you are hoping to win it from a person. So let's again try to understand how the majority of people behave in their day-to-day lives.

When normal people go shopping, let's say to purchase an item of clothing, they go into a shop and look for the item in question. When they have found something they quite like, their next impulse is to check the price tag. I find it so frustrating when people come to me and present their services or products without disclosing the fees or price. This subject is covered in more detail in the next chapter.

So let's go back to the preparation of a proposal/quotation. The first page of a document should clearly state in very positive terminology exactly the results that your product or service will achieve for your prospect. Focus not on what the product or service is, but on what it will do. This means you have got to stick your neck out and make promises to the prospective client. If you are afraid of doing that, you shouldn't be offering your product or service in the marketplace. Remember, it is the result that your client will be buying.

Let me now go to the last page of your document. This should clearly state the costs. In between the first and last page you will supply the detail. It should preferably be in plain language, and if you want it to be read, in short paragraphs. This content really is the what, the how and the when. The document must also reflect your brand image, so it should feel and look professional, and be a sign of quality. For example, the cover could have your company or firm's logo on one side and your prospect's company or firm logo on the other.

A Proposal

Specifically

Prepared

For

(the company name)

Now let's move into the actual presentation. You arrive, go through the normal greetings, then give a short recap of what you understand the requirements to be. This now focuses the presentee's mind. It also highlights any misunderstanding immediately. Then move on to the presentation itself. Hand the document over and say, 'Let me take you through this.' Go straight to page 1 and talk it through. After completing the first page, check with the other person:

Are you happy with what I am saying so far?

Is this what you wanted?

Have we got this bit right?

If you get an agreement, take the person straight to the back page. Preface it by saying something like:

I hope you will be delighted with the price.

I/we have got a really good price for you.

I am pleased to say that this is an excellent price.

I think you will find that this is outstanding value for money.

Then check that the prospect agrees, by asking, 'Is this OK?' Be prepared to talk about money. If you reach a reasonable consensus, you can then move into the main detail of the document. It is always advisable to have one or two case histories (stories) that you can relay during this meeting.

When you have gone through the document, check again with your prospect:

Are you happy with this now?

Do you see how our... will help you to achieve...?

Is there anything else you would like to ask me?

In the final stage of the presentation your objective is to make it easy for your prospect to do business with you. In the profession of selling this is often referred to as closing. There are still a range of closing techniques being taught by trainers, but they have passed their sell-by date. Come on, let's get real. Do you yourself want to be 'closed' when you are considering buying something? You almost certainly do not. What your prospect would appreciate is help in making the right decision.

So assuming the other person indicates he or she is comfortable with what you have presented, your final statement should be:

If this is OK, now let's complete the paperwork.

Now you will get either a yes or one of many variables.

I need to discuss this with someone else.

One possible reply is, 'Fine. I quite understand that. Do you mind my asking when you plan to do that?' Wait for an answer, then say 'OK, I'll give you a call on....'

I don't want to make a decision today.

Your reply could be, 'Sure. That's OK. When would you like me to phone you?' If the person answers, 'No, I'll call you,' your response might be, 'It would save a lot of time if I phone you, as I work on an outgoing diary. So can I call you on...?' Here you fix a date and time. (Nobody else knows what an outgoing diary is, and nor do I – but it serves the purpose of keeping you in control!)

The second type of presentation is to a group, perhaps a board of directors. In these opportunities it is advisable to use a laptop, preferably connected to a small projector. If your prospect expects a number of people to be in attendance, there will normally be a screen available. You must also take a hard copy of the presentation with you, based upon the example described previously, to be handed out at the conclusion of the spoken presentation. It you hand it out beforehand, the audience will read it and will not concentrate on your presentation or listen to what you are saying.

There are a number of tips in helping you to prepare a winning PowerPoint presentation:

- Make your points using short bullets, not paragraphs.
- Each bullet point must roll up individually and consecutively.
- Include your company's logo and the prospect company's logo in the corners of each slide.
- If possible include one or two visuals to make the presentation more interesting.

There are six stages of a successful presentation:

1. First of all, show the results, what you will achieve for the prospect with your product or service, because this is the most important part. If they like the results the price becomes less of a barrier. Again, once you have presented the results, pause and check that everyone is in agreement.

2. Now go to prices and fees, and endeavour to get a reaction.

3. Now go into the detail, but not too much of it. Again use bullet points. The detail should be more fully covered in the document.

4. If applicable, give one or two case histories showing what you have achieved for others. These must be relevant to your prospect's needs.

5. Now provide something to give you credibility. You could perhaps mention past or existing clients, possibly showing their company logo.

6. Finally, outline your guarantee (the risk reversal, away from the prospect and onto your organization).

I am often asked how long these sorts of presentation should last. There really is no firm rule, but as a guideline, 30 minutes of presenting time is sufficient. There will always be questions and discussion. It is best of all to set out the rules before you start presenting, using one of these wordings:

> I shall be making a presentation which will last for roughly 30 minutes. I would be very grateful if you could save your questions until the end.
>
> As I am presenting, if you have questions just raise them at any time.

The success of this type of presentation really depends on the skills of the presenter. I have had the experience of listening to a presenter who has not been trained, and no doubt you have as well. I get very frustrated in this situation: it can be an awful experience. Just about every executive these days is required to make a presentation or give a speech from time to time, so for goodness' sake, get some speaker training. There can be no excuse for not doing it properly. If you need some help on this subject email success@denny.co.uk.

Public speaking probably causes more stress to the untrained person than any other business activity. People are afraid of drying up, of making a hash of it, of being asked questions they can't answer, and so on and so on. Some people suffer with such terrible nerves that they physically shake. All of these problems are easily rectifiable if you prepare well and are confident of what you are saying.

So there it is: a presentation is easy to deliver if it is well researched and planned. At the conclusion, take control again. Ask the group, 'How do you feel?' Always be mindful of your audience's body language and facial expressions. You will easily spot those who disapprove. If it seems that most people are happy, ask, 'What is the next step?' Now revert to the previous examples for advice on how to proceed from here.

Presenting should be fun, delivered with a smile and enthusiasm. Please don't bang on about yourself or your company. The audience will not be particularly interested in you or your company. And they certainly are not buying your company (unless it is for sale). They are buying what you can do for them.

I personally like to conclude every meeting of this kind with this type of phraseology:

> Thank you. From my side this has been a good meeting. May I ask you, has it achieved what you wanted to achieve?

Questions are great, but if you are not sure what is being asked, to reduce any misunderstanding always ask it back.

> I am sorry. Exactly what do you mean by that?

> I am so sorry. I don't quite understand.

If you don't know the answer to a question, never make an answer up. Admit that you don't know. Be aware that some comments are not questions, they are statements. On other occasions, if the question is a really good one, you can build your relationship by saying, 'That is a really good point.'

This very short example can be used as a basis for every type of meeting you ever have. It leaves everything on a positive note.

Pocket Reminders

- Explain the results of your product or service.
- Be enthusiastic about your fees or price.
- Be pleased to be asked questions. It shows interest.
- Use visuals.
- Give yourself some credibility.
- Make it easy for the prospect to proceed.

Wise words

The error of the past is the wisdom and success of the future.

10

'Priceitis' is for Nerds

I have been fortunate in advising numerous companies over the years on their selling operation. Our training consultants and I have trained literally thousands of people in the skills of professional salesmanship. We have discovered a disease suffered by the non-achieving sales person, which we call 'priceitis'.

It manifests itself in this way. The seller goes out on a hot lead and later returns to the office with a despondent tale to tell. He or she proceeds to tell the boss, 'That was a bum lead. What a waste of time. We would have got some business if only we were cheaper. Our prices are too high. We just aren't competitive enough.' The sales person has convinced him- or herself that everyone else is cheaper. This poor soul now needs some serious treatment to cure this malady. He or she will become redundant sooner or later unless it can be cured fast.

Sales people may truly believe, and convince themselves, that in order to win new business their offer has to be the cheapest. So let's be completely realistic. If it was the case in both business to consumer and business to business sales that people only ever bought the cheapest, the role of the sales person would be totally redundant. Nobody in the business to business sector would need to employ sales people: all that was needed would be price lists and a distribution method.

In the business to consumer sector, the white and black goods retailers know it is definitely not the case that the consumer buys the cheapest. As a result many retailers are upskilling their floor staff to have greater product knowledge, and to be able to explain the features and benefits of their products, which in turn justify the price.

The role of the professional sales person is to be able to win business when the product or service is not the cheapest, and that is why excellent companies invest in upskilling their sales people with professional selling skills.

Now let's stay real. Do people buy the cheapest? Of course they do. Up until the mid-1990s approximately 18 per cent of people, in both the business to business and business to consumer markets, bought the cheapest. This has now risen to approximately 25 per cent. At the other extreme, do people buy the most expensive? Yes, they do – approximately 4 per cent of them.

One of the clients we worked with was Dunhill. (This is not the cigarettes: that brand was sold to Rothmans many years ago. The Dunhill brand is now used to market high-quality merchandise from clothes to luggage, and from watches to fragrances.) On my last visit to the flagship shop in Bond Street, London, I noticed that the cheapest men's belt on sale was £119. Nevertheless, Dunhill sell a lot of belts. I am sure they are outstanding belts, of better quality than those of most other retailers. But if we are totally basic about it, the purpose of a belt is to hold your trousers up. That does not demand that you spend £119: a piece of string would do it. But people like beautiful, high-quality Dunhill belts. This illustrates once again that people will always find the money for what they really want.

Now if we return to the statistic that 25 per cent of people buy the cheapest and 4 per cent buy the most expensive, what do the remaining 71 per cent buy? They buy perceived *value for money*. So therefore it must make sense that this is the big market and the big opportunity. I am quite certain that many of my readers who are in manufacturing will question this logic, particularly with the demise of so much of the manufacturing industry that used to be found in the British industrial heartland, but has now moved to the Far East.

But let me challenge you. Is the cheapest car the biggest seller? Is the cheapest supermarket the supermarket with the biggest growth? And what about the cheapest clothes? Now let's turn to the professionals. Are the cheapest lawyers the largest firms? How about the accountants, the architects and the vets? It is as I said earlier: you must match the brand to the customer profile or the customers you want to have.

In my own sector, is the cheapest training company the most successful, or the cheapest executive recruitment agency the most profitable? Of course not. Statistically it seems that the businesses that go into liquidation are the ones that were cheapest. There is a market for cheapness, but as we all know, pile it high and sell it cheap is a strategy that carries a big, big risk. Why? Quite obviously, it's because there is not sufficient profit for reinvestment. But we must stay completely realistic here, and be aware of trading patterns.

There are two reasons that the proportion of people looking for cheapness has gone from 18 per cent to 25 per cent. The first is cheap air travel and the second is the internet. I used to fly regularly from Birmingham to Edinburgh on a flagship carrier. The return price was £220. Then the budget airlines came into being, and they were able to offer the same three-quarters of an hour journey for a return price of £50. Like many others, I immediately started to use them. We have since seen the incredible growth of air travel, with people being more price conscious and the movement of market share on short-haul flights to the cost cutters.

But then the flag carriers fought back and reduced their prices. At the time I am writing this book, a flagship carrier charges £20 more than a budget airline for the flight from Birmingham to Edinburgh. Some of the budget airlines do not provide customer satisfaction. The planes and seats are getting dirtier. The passengers are more cramped. Baggage gets delayed and the planes are sometimes not on time. This is where value for money kicks in. If there is a massive price difference, the 71 per cent are not stupid in avoiding the expensive option. But if the price difference is fairly small, people go where they see value for money.

As far as the internet is concerned, I am not clever enough, nor am I able to read sufficiently into the future, to know where this type of trading will go. All I do know is that more and more people are using the internet for their purchasing. At the same time the market is growing, in all sectors. We all know that we can save between £5,000 and £10,000 on the purchase of a new car through the internet. But has that devastated retail motor dealers? No, it has not. Why? Because there is an element of fear: people want to know and trust the person who sells them a large, expensive item. They want after-sales care and so on. Again this illustrates the importance of value for money.

So, my readers, this is a big opportunity. Tell your prospects:

We provide excellent value for money.

Our services are great value for money.

Now let's go to the prevention of 'priceitis'.

Be proud of your prices!

Let's take the scenario. You go shopping. You go into a shop and see that it has some really great gear. You find something that appeals to you, and your next move is to look for the price tag. If it is not priced, you more than likely think that the tag has fallen off. So you check out other items, and discover that nothing is priced. Instantly your mind is conditioned to believe that these items are very expensive. You probably walk out and continue down the high street. You glance into an antique shop window and see that all of the price tags are upside down. You move on further down the high street and you see a big sign in a shop window 'SPECIAL PRICE £50' in very big letters. You are more than likely to pause to investigate.

The first thing a retailer does when it holds a sale is to put big price tags on the sale items. What this is really saying is, 'Today we are proud of our prices.' But, this implies, 'Last week we were ripping you off.' Our brains have been conditioned to believe that if people are proud of their prices, we are getting better value for money. So always be upfront with your prices, and when you reply to the 'how much?', give your answer with an element of enthusiasm.

In all probability one of the stupidest mistakes made by people endeavouring to win new business is not to price match. I find it very embarrassing when somebody tries to sell me something I can't afford. I may want it but I really can't afford it. This may sound in conflict with what I have already said, that people will generally find the money for the things that they really want – but the difference here is in the word *really*.

It also depends on how big the mismatch on price actually is. For example, if you have a budget of £500,000 to buy a new house, you would not be looking at houses in the £750,000 price bracket. But if you found a house that you really, really wanted and it was priced at £560,000, you would more than likely borrow the extra money required.

This is such an important area in business. It is important to grasp it fully. From the business winner's prospective it is called price conditioning.

Another example. I wanted a new telecommunications system that would connect my home and my office. A British Telecoms sales person called on me. I told him what I wanted. After about an hour of visiting the site and discussion, he said, 'Let me give you a quotation.' The quote was approximately £2,500. I said, 'Thank you, and on your bike.' (I wasn't actually that rude: I said, 'Thank you, and I will think about it.') You see, in my mind was a price of about £500. If he had had the courtesy to ask me whether I had a budget or a price in mind, I more than likely would have said £400 – leaving a bit of leeway, as we all do in these circumstances. The sales person would have reckoned he could sell me the right product for possibly £500 or £600. About a week after this incident I called into a BT outlet, and discovered it did have a system which was fairly basic but suited my purpose, for £570. If only that original engineer had been skilled on price conditioning, he could have sold it to me. So please, my readers, don't be afraid to talk money. It is not a dirty subject. It is what makes the world go round.

Just step into the other person's shoes and try to understand what he or she is thinking. This is so easy to do, if you ask simple, sensible questions:

Have you a price in mind?

Do you have a budget?

Do you mind me asking you, how much are you allocating for...?

I obviously would like to do business with you. Can you give me an indication of how much you would like to spend?

There is a tendency in our current trading environment for an element of negotiation to take place. Particularly in business to business transactions, my people and I are often asked for a discount. Alternatively we get the price objection, so let's deal with this first. When a person says, 'The price is too high,' you cannot find the right response without knowing more, because it has too many meanings. It could mean:

Somebody else is cheaper.

It is more expensive than I thought it would be.

I can't afford it.

I want a discount.

It is outside my budget.

I am not the decision maker.

It's my job to reduce the price.

I don't really want it.

When someone says the price is too high, it could mean any of these things. The first step in handling that statement is to respond with a question, in order for you to find the real and genuine meaning:

In relation to what?

How much is too much?

May I ask you why you say that?

That's an interesting point. Do you mind me asking you why you think it is too high?

Once you have found out the real concern, it then becomes relatively easy to deal with.

The process of negotiation starts with preventing the business winner from succumbing to the temptation to be a *price crumbler*. When a prospect is attempting to reduce your price, this is where negotiation should kick in – and the principle of good negotiation is to trade concessions. Here is an example:

> Mr/Ms..., if you agree to pay half now and the balance in 14 days, then we can meet your price.

> We just don't have sufficient margin to drop the price. But what I can provide is... (mention an extra service that will be of real value to your prospect) if you agree to take the package.

The skilled negotiator always has something to trade that is not the price. If you sell your product or service correctly, you will have inflamed the prospect's desire for it, but he or she will still want to negotiate the best possible deal. Try never to get into a haggling situation over prices. If you sense that your price is near enough to what your prospect has been conditioned to expect, then negotiate the variables. They should be cheap to you but valuable to your prospective customer.

Make a list of the concessions you are prepared to make. Here is a list of questions you should ask yourself to help you to compile your own list:

- What do we normally make?
- What are they worth?
- What can we receive in exchange?
- What other variables do we have?
- What can we offer that is cheap to us but valuable to the prospect?
- What can prospects offer us that is cheap to them but valuable to us?

Be miserly. This is perhaps one of the most important principles of good negotiation, especially if you intend to build a long-term relationship. There is nothing more uncomfortable for both buyer and seller than when the seller agrees too readily on a negotiated package. I am sure that you must have experienced this yourself when you have had something to sell. You advertise your house, car or whatever, and the buyer makes you an offer which you immediately accept. The buyer goes away thinking, 'I should have made a lower offer. I'll bet he would have accepted it.' You are left thinking, 'I should have got a better deal. I am sure he would have paid more if I had stuck it out.'

If you are going to trade concessions, you must trade them reluctantly. You must put up a fight at every stage: every concession must be wrung out of you. When people reach an agreement too quickly, both parties always feel that they could have got a better deal. The next time they will negotiate a much tougher one. So don't ever say 'Yes' too quickly. Don't ever accept the first offer. You must always feel that you really have negotiated a good deal. So whenever you are about to say 'Yes', say 'No' just a few more times.

The result of a good negotiation should never be a winner and a loser. Both parties should feel just slightly dissatisfied. This is so important if you want a long-term relationship.

Whenever I am now asked the discount question, I always respond with another question. 'Do you mind my asking why you want a discount?' Again, until you hear the reply to that question you cannot respond effectively. The current market-place is more monetarily aware than ever, as we all know. People are more willing to discuss and negotiate in order to get the best value for money.

So let's be absolutely clear. You must defend your price. Don't give into pressure for a discount unless you are exchanging it for quantity or faster payment. Useful phrases to use are:

We consider it dishonest to sell to one person at one price and to another at a different price.

If we felt that this is a fair price, why would we want to give you a different price?

My final words on this subject are – be proud of your price.

Pocket Reminders

- Offer value for money.
- Be proud of your prices.
- Don't catch 'priceitis'.
- Always price condition.
- Don't be a price crumbler.
- Negotiation means trading concessions.

Wise words

Great minds have purpose. Others have wishes.

11

The Big Opportunity

You don't need to have the best products or the best services, but if you provide an outstanding customer service you are going to win and win and win. Tom Peters, one of the greatest management gurus in the business world, claims that 'it is the greatest secret in the global economy that if you can provide awesome customer care, you will need new suitcases to carry all of the money home.'

One of the most popular presentations I am asked to give around the world is entitled 'Profit from customer care.' If you harness this opportunity, you will most certainly build your business with a solid future. Very few people, from captains of industry to front-line employees, really understand what customer care is.

I get so frustrated when I read the statement in corporate literature, 'We pride ourselves on our service.' The boardrooms of those companies are having little pride sessions, but I wonder what their customers really think. Let me give you an example. Your car goes in for its 10,000 mile service. You go to collect it, it is ready on time, and every single detail of the manufacturer's checklist has been carried out. The bill that you are now presented with is exactly what you were quoted in the first place. If this were to happen you might be tempted to say,

'What good service.' In actual fact there is zero service and zero customer care. All the garage has done is to do the job for which you are going to pay.

So let's see where good service and customer care kicks in. Take the same scenario. Your car goes in for its service. It's ready on time, all the works have been carried out and the invoice is correct, but on top of that the car has been washed. The inside has been vacuumed, there is a clean sheet of white paper in the footwell, and maybe a bunch of flowers or small box of chocolates on the passenger seat. You may well laugh, but these little extras are what make the difference.

It would be so easy for conveyancing lawyers when their clients move into their new homes to send them a bottle of champagne or a plant for the garden. The cost is small but the goodwill is priceless.

Very few businesses actually achieve what the customer is paying for, but getting that right is no qualification for saying, 'We pride ourselves on our service.' Getting it right means that you deserve to get paid. That alone is not the vital ingredient for maximizing the big opportunity that comes from customer care.

I always find it very amusing when banks announce a new service to their customers. This in all honesty is fraudulent, because what they are really doing is putting out a new product which will no doubt become a new income stream. The people who live in their ivory towers are unable to distinguish between a product and a service.

So before you even really commence the approach to the 'big one' (customer care, or CC), check your own business procedures. Are you delivering the right goods or services to the right people on time? Do you keep strictly to every commitment? In other words, if you promise to make a particular call at a given time, do you do it? If you have promised a letter by a certain deadline, do you adhere to that promise? There is a frightful tendency in every aspect of business for people to over-promise and under-deliver. All this achieves is customer dissatisfaction.

People over-promise in their promotional material or in their attempt to win a new client, and then the delivery doesn't come up to the expectation of the client. Instead of gaining an ambassador they have gained an enemy, and more than likely 5 or 10 more in the process. As we all know, people will tell several others when they feel let down or have suffered from what they call bad service. On the other hand when they have what is called good service – that is, the product meets their expectations – they rarely share this with others. All that has been achieved is a satisfied customer. However, if you deliver awesome customer care you have an ambassador who will certainly tell at least two others, and this can be an incredibly inexpensive way of winning new clients or customers.

Currently, business people are responding to short-termism. This is caused by expectations of immediate results from shareholders. Shareholders want profits now and not in three or four years' time. In turn this cascades into almost every type of business. Get it now. Do it now. Achieve the figures now. Meet the target. Achieve the budget. Very little thought is given to lifetime customer value.

Let me tell you another short story. My wife had a friend who had been going to a particular hairdresser for 10 years. Latterly she had been having her hair coloured as well as cut there, and her average spend now worked out at approximately £20 per week. She didn't have her hair coloured every week, but she did go every week for it to be restyled, so it averaged out at about £20. The day prior to this woman's colouring appointment, the hairdresser received a big promotion from the colourant manufacturer Wella. It took away the old range of hair colourants on a special deal, and supplied the hairdresser with a new range. The following day our friend turned up for her colouring appointment. The hairdresser announced with enthusiasm that he had a new range of colours. Our friend said she didn't want to change from her existing colour. The hairdresser said the new colours were very similar to the old ones. Our friend said they might well be, but she did not wish to change. The hairdresser replied, 'I'm sorry, but the old colour is no longer available.' (In fact the old range was still on the market, and he could have easily obtained the colour she wanted.) So she said, 'Oh well, never mind. I'll leave it today.' And off she went. She duly found another hairdresser who stocked her original tint.

Let's just look at this illustration: £20 per week is roughly £1,000 per year. I know from the age of our friend that she would have carried on going to the hairdresser for at least another 10 years, and possibly 20. She had already been going there for 10 years. Imagine if I walked into the hairdresser at the end of that day and said to him, 'You've just lost a customer who was worth between £10,000 and £20,000 to you.' No doubt he would have been flabbergasted and distraught. Isn't it amazing how few business people fail to understand the importance of *lifetime customer value?* I hope you will never make this mistake.

I was recently given some research on why customers quit. My first example is taken from the banking sector. It is based upon these issues.

Complaints leading to a threat to close an account

- 67 per cent policy reasons;
- 17 per cent people reasons;
- 12 per cent process reasons;
- 3 per cent product reasons;
- 1 per cent premises reasons.

As you have no doubt noticed, the main reason for customers leaving a bank is bank policy. These are policies that have been created by people totally divorced from the real world and the customer. They come out with a new-fangled policy that the branch staff are expected to deliver. It might achieve an increased short-term profit, but it will certainly achieve customer dissatisfaction and a dislike for the brand.

The second example is based on research across a wide range of businesses.

Why customers don't return

- 1 per cent die;
- 3 per cent move away;
- 5 per cent have other contacts;
- 9 per cent competitive reasons;
- 14 per cent product dissatisfaction;
- 68 per cent indifference by staff.

Now I don't know what you have gleaned from the above. But when I first saw these statistics I have to confess that I was really excited. You really can't stop your customers dying. You can't prevent them from moving away. You can't stop them having other contacts, and you cannot control your competitors. But you can do something about product dissatisfaction, and you are certainly able to do something about the 68 per cent of staff indifference. Isn't this a fantastic opportunity?

All you have to do here is to develop a customer care culture. Treat others as you would like to be treated. Keep your promises. All members of staff, whether they are customer-facing or not, must realize that they are part of the culture. Delivering, meeting and exceeding customer expectations depends on everyone in a business supporting each other, helping each other, rather than the attitude of 'This is not my job – I am not paid to do that.'

What is your telephone manner like? Are your clients or customers pleased to call you? Does everybody in your organization set out to be helpful, interested and, above all, caring?

If you do a lot of business, realistically from time to time you will have a customer complaint. If you don't get any complaints, you either don't do much business or you fib about other things as well. The most destructive barrier to developing a customer care culture is a blame culture. This starts at the top. A customer complains – and as we all know the majority of people don't like complaining, but from time to time they are forced into doing it. The boss or manager then proceeds to find someone to carry the can, and he or she no doubt gets a good ticking off.

I earnestly suggest that you develop a 'welcome complaints' culture, a culture that demonstrates throughout that you are pleased to get a complaint. Why? Because, quite simply, this is an opportunity. First, if it is handled well, you can turn a complaining customer into an ambassador. Second, it gives you an opportunity to correct and improve the procedure that caused the complaint.

This is one of our areas of speciality in working with all types of businesses, and helping them to change from a product or process-driven culture to a customer-led culture. We did an experiment with one client. This particular company was a huge European supplier of stationery, an extremely competitive industry. In order to hold on to its margins, the company's USP (unique selling point) was to provide outstanding customer care.

The experiment went like this. The company selected its top 1,000 customers and contacted them, saying that if they had cause for a complaint, they should notify the company immediately and they would be given £100. At the end of a two-year period the company had received 127 complaints. It knew seven of them were fraudulent but nonetheless it paid up. A further five were questionable. The remainder were genuine, and in the majority of cases fairly minor. The company analysed every complaint, treating each one as an opportunity to improve its processes. The staff said to me that it was one of the most cost-effective exercises they had ever carried out.

I am not advocating that you should do this, I am merely using it as an example to illustrate the benefits of welcoming complaints. Let me briefly give you the procedure for handling a customer complaint:

1. Once you receive a complaint it must take priority over every single other activity.

2. Find out exactly what the complaint is by asking questions. How? When? What? This is to make sure that there is no misunderstanding.

3. Find out the customer's expectation. In other words, do not offer a solution until you find out exactly what the customer wants, or else you will be in further trouble with a mismatch. You must meet exactly what the customer wants here. If customers want their money back, give it. If they want a replacement, do it – fast. So the question you ask is this:

How can I put this right?

What would you like me to do about it?

4. Then follow up when you have carried out the request by making sure your customer is now happy.

Customer care is really about doing more than was expected, rather than just enough to get by. It is therefore worthwhile to break down how customer care can be delivered. There are two areas.

The first is the *tangible*. This is the area where you spend money on your customers. It can include everything from corporate entertainment to give-aways – from taking a client out to lunch to a Christmas card. Many businesses can't even get the latter right. Last Christmas, when the Christmas cards arrived at my office we divided them into three categories. The first type of card had no signature at all, only the company name. They went straight into the charity box. The second beneficiary to the charity were cards that had anything up to 10 signatures on them. You can imagine that everyone was asked to sign but they hadn't a clue who the card was going to. The third demonstrated, 'I care about you.' These cards were personalized by a handwritten message and a signature.

The second area of customer care is the *intangible*, which costs nothing other than a tiny amount of time and a little thought. Let me tell you another story. I was on the M25 one morning (for those of you who are not familiar with this motorway, it is known as the biggest car park in Europe), stuck in the usual traffic jam and listening to the Radio Four news programme *Today*. One of our old clients, Alan Jones, was being interviewed. At that time he was managing director of TNT, the international haulers. When TNT first arrived in the United Kingdom (it is an Australian company) we carried out a lot of training for it, but we had lost contact as a result of our own neglect. The following day I sent Alan a letter, which basically said, 'I heard you on the radio yesterday. It was a great interview and you came across really well. It brightened up my journey while I was stuck in a traffic jam on the M25.'

A few days late I received a reply, 'Dear Richard, How nice to hear from you after all this time. I am so glad to hear that you are still in business. [I wasn't too sure about that.] I am sending you under separate cover a book on the freight industry that has just been published. The TNT story is in it. I thought you might like to have it.'

I duly responded. 'Dear Alan, Thank you so much for your book. I am really looking forward to reading it. I am sending you under separate cover a copy of my book *Selling to Win*.' Approximately 10 days later our office received a phone call from the marketing manager of TNT. He asked us to give him a price for 400 of our books, which we did. The order was delivered and the relationship started all over again.

There is an old saying, 'It's not what you know but who you know that is important.' This is a completely useless saying. Now let me give you the power saying. 'It's not what you know or who you know, it's what you do with who you know that's important.' We have all met name-droppers, and they are all rather a waste of space. So how can you use this golden snippet? Look for the opportunity to send a caring note, maybe a handwritten card – not an e-mail – congratulating someone you've met before on his or her achievements. If you are reading trade magazines, newspapers or the local paper, and you recognize or have met a person who is featured, send him or her a congratulatory note. One of the laws of success (taken from my book *Succeed for Yourself*) is what you hand out in life, you get back. You can get back a tenfold return.

Target yourself to make one contact a week that demonstrates you care about someone. If you want your customers to care about you, it starts with you caring about them.

Intangible customer care is the follow-up phone call. It is showing concern. It is doing something that you didn't have to do. My last example was told to me by Michael Bache of the giant Federal Express company. When FedEx started out, it had the idea of delivering the right parcels to the right people, on time every time. It had developed software that could track a parcel throughout its journey. It started off with a few depots in the United States. On the first week of trading the company transported about 40 parcels. On the second week the number grew to around 60, so it wasn't doing very well. One of the depots had a call from one of its customers on a Friday afternoon to say that her parcel hadn't arrived. The lady who took the call apologized, and enquired whether it was important. The customer replied, 'Yes, very important. It contains my wedding dress and I'm getting married tomorrow.' The lady in the depot said, 'I understand. Leave it with me.' She went to find her boss, but he was out on business calls. She then thought, what am I going to do? She stepped into the customer's shoes and realized that if she was getting married and hadn't received her wedding dress she would be devastated. She set out to discover where the parcel was. It turned out to be over a thousand miles away, and there was no chance of getting it to the customer on time by the normal FedEx service. She got on the phone, found an airplane charter company, and hired a small Cessna. The parcel was collected and duly delivered, and the driver told the story.

Meanwhile back in the office, the call-taker's boss returned, and she told him what she had just done. As you can imagine he wasn't best pleased to discover how much it had cost to fix this problem. The woman's reply was, 'Well, we are going to go bust anyhow, so let's go out with a big bang.' The following Monday morning the first phone call they had in the office was from the customer, calling from Mexico on her honeymoon. She said how grateful she was, but added jokingly that she wasn't very happy because she had told the story at her reception of how FedEx had got her wedding dress to her. Apparently everyone talked about the delivery rather than her dress! It so happened that there were two very senior executives from huge corporations attending the reception. One of them was from RCA. The following day RCA switched to FedEx, and it has never looked back from that day to this.

Now I am not suggesting that you deliver your products or services by Cessna. I am suggesting however that customer care is the big opportunity.

Pocket Reminders

- Distinguish between doing the job and customer care.
- Ban a blame culture.
- Do more than is expected.
- Under-promise and over-deliver.
- Send out one caring note a week.
- Praise your staff when they go the extra mile.

Wise words

Courage is not the absence of fear but acting in the face of it.

12

The Right Balance

There is a new word that has already been recorded in the *Oxford English Dictionary*, affluenza. Briefly, it comes from the idea that in our Western culture many people are rich, but they are not experiencing fulfilment, contentment, peace of mind and what could loosely be called happiness. Affluenza is a kind of disease, caused by too much money and too little fulfilment.

This condition is caused by the pressures of a consumer society, where we are all striving for material achievements. We all know that more people are wealthy than ever before, and that as well as money in the bank they have cars, property, boats, airplanes and luxury items. The percentage of the population classified as millionaires has rocketed in the last four to five years. Some of the wealthiest people are now in nations that formerly were regarded as among the poorest, such as China, India and Russia.

In the United States and Europe there has been, and still is, a culture of striving for wealth and affluence. The old saying of 'keeping up with the Jones' is more pertinent now than ever before. But has this greater affluence brought greater peace of mind and contentment? Apparently not. It has not fulfilled our spiritual needs, and our values and relationships have suffered.

Our most valuable asset is our brain (I know I am being repetitive), and it is being put under too much pressure and stress. When I was a young man, stress counselling was unheard of – it just didn't happen that people were hospitalized with stress-related illnesses. The balance of life has gone wrong. Having millions in the bank, cars, boats, planes and beautiful houses is all very well, but is it really all worth it if there is nobody to share those possessions with, or if the kids are in trouble and despise their parents?

To state the obvious, we are all on this planet for such a short time, and we can't take our possessions with us when we go. Each one of us must accept the responsibility to correct and then manage the balance in our lives. We have a duty to both ourselves and our loved ones to do this. I said earlier that the purpose of work for most of us is to earn the money to pay for that part of life that is important. I fully accept and respect that many people find their whole purpose in life in dedication to others. They are the exception, though, and they almost certainly are not the readers of this book.

If our most valuable asset is our brain, it is a priority to give it some attention. The brain needs oxygen to function well. We have all been told that regular exercise is a must, because it helps not only to prevent but also to cure stress-related problems, depression being one. So just be honest with yourself, and admit there is no excuse for not taking some form of regular exercise. You need it to keep your body and your brain in peak condition. It really is a question of priorities. To claim that you don't have the time is the feeblest and weakest of all excuses. It is our responsibility to manage our brain, and our time, effectively.

The idea of affluenza is that our spiritual needs are being neglected. Some people are fortunate in having a religion or belief that becomes their bedrock. Now I am not advocating that you instantly take up a religion. It is fine for some, but not compulsory. But what we can all do is get our values right.

Getting the values right depends on having a philosophy for life. We should all stand back from our day-to-day work and pressures, and ask ourselves, what is our purpose? What is our life for? And really question ourselves on what will genuinely make us happy.

There are three guaranteed ways of creating greater joy and happiness. First, make someone else happy. It is virtually impossible not to gain joy, happiness and inner satisfaction when you are enhancing someone else's life. This can be as simple as a smile, a compliment or even a kind word.

Second, we must all understand that the majority of people need to share in some form or another. I don't know of anybody with a magnificent house, with a stunning car parked outside, with a beautiful boat in a marina, who lives on their own with no one to share this affluence with, who is truly happy and contented with their life.

Now you may be getting the impression that I am against affluence. Nothing could be further from the truth. I respect and admire ambition. I respect all those people in the world who have achieved great wealth honestly and morally, as without question they have helped countless of thousands of others in the process. The point that is so obvious is that it is necessary to manage the balance.

Third, human beings do best when they have something to look forward to. We see from the news programmes on our television screens the dreadful events that take place around the world, from earthquakes to starvation, and from poverty to human conflict. The sights of human carnage are of course horrendously distressing, but surely the worst sight of all is a face without hope. We must have hope. It is our duty and our responsibility to be looking forward and not backward. It is all very well for me to say this sitting in the comfort of my library when I have only just mentioned disasters, but most of you, my readers, are not suffering from a major natural disaster. So there really is no reason why you shouldn't have something that you are looking forward to doing or experiencing. To put it another way, you should be setting goals.

In Chapter 3 I mentioned singer-songwriter Sheryl Crow, and her song 'Soak up the sun', which says that it's not having what you want, it's wanting what you have that's important. So many people seem to think the grass is greener on the other side of the hedge, but thinking that is not the way to fulfilment. Let me tell you a story.

There was a rancher in California in 1847 who owned a sizeable ranch. Hearing that gold had been discovered in southern California, he sold his ranch to a Colonel Sutter and went off to search for gold, never to return. Colonel Sutter built a mill on the stream that ran through the ranch. One day his little girl brought into the house some wet sand from the mill's raceway. She placed it before the fire to dry, and as she was sifting the sand through her fingers, a visitor noticed the first shining scales of real gold ever discovered in that part of California. Those few acres yielded gold worth $38 million in a very short period of time. Apparently, at the height of production, $120 worth of gold was extracted every 15 minutes. If only the original rancher had realized what he already owned.

There is a great message here for us all. Let's be thankful and happy with what we've already got, and then let's discover how we can make more of what we have learnt and achieved so far.

I am sure you are already successful, but nevertheless you would like to enhance your affluence for yourself and for your loved ones, or you would not be reading this book. Let me state right away that you have the power within you to do just that. Your most valuable asset, your brain, has untold capabilities. Its full potential is still untapped. All it needs is some motivation, and the belief that you can get what you really want.

Again let's be realistic. It would be really stupid to say that we can all achieve everything we want. We can't. What we can unquestionably achieve is what we *really* want. To achieve this you must have goals.

The extraordinary thing about goals is that so few people actually do decide what they want. You've no doubt heard the phrase, 'A person who is going nowhere normally gets there.' It is quite extraordinary when you ask people what they want, to realize how very few *really* do know what they want. People talk in glib terms of 'I want to be successful' or 'I'd like to be a millionaire,' but they actually haven't a clue, and are unhappy because they haven't got they don't know what.

It is said that 'what the mind of man can accurately conceive and believe it is forced to achieve'. The history of humankind has been a history of goal achievement. Leading psychologists now regard the brain and the nervous system as a highly complex automatic goal-seeking mechanism. So we all have the equipment necessary to achieve what we really want, if we care to use it.

Make a list of all the things you really want, both long term and short term, in your business life and in your private life. Include both tangible and intangible wants. In making this list you must be realistic. I have heard motivational speakers tell their audiences to 'set big goals'. They are wrong, and it can be dangerous. It may sound highly motivational in a convention hall, but the danger is that short-term goals that are too big don't become believable and are therefore not achieved. Big goals should be set long term. Whatever you do, don't put down monetary goals. The more a person chases money, the more likely it is to run away. The goal must be tangible. I do not know of any millionaires who set out with the main aim of making a million. The millions came as a by-product of their goals.

Intangible goals can be in the areas of personal development: getting fit, losing weight, becoming a leader not a manager, being a good communicator and so on. While you are thinking about personal goals I strongly advise you to discuss this with your partner if you have one. Both of you no doubt will have some different goals, and there is nothing wrong with that as long as you have some goals that you share. Two people pulling together become a powerful force.

Now I am quite certain that some of my readers will have difficulty in doing this. If you find it hard, it could well be a result of your upbringing or your environment. I have met many cynics of personal development over the years. They decry the so-called self-help books and personal development programmes. The majority of those folk have got their arse hanging out of their trousers! But I have never met a person who is self-made (it is only they who admit it) who will decry anything that helps people enhance their lives.

Just setting some goals does not mean that they will be achieved with certainty. May I remind you of the law of success, which states that it is desire, not ability, that determines our success. I have heard of numerous examples of young people who were not high academic achievers in school, and even some instances where they were classified as failures and dropouts, and left school with no academic qualifications. After having had a job or two, they found a career or a job opportunity that they really wanted, but it called for an academic qualification. So they returned to formal education, took the exams that they had previously failed, and this time passed with flying colours. Had their ability changed? Certainly not. It was their desire. In order to build desire the brain must have something that it really wants to achieve, which is of course a goal.

So select from your list of goals one that you will make your primary goal. This goal must be:

■ set high enough to be worth achieving;
■ achievable in months, not years – ideally within a maximum of three months;
■ realistic, if there are any financial considerations.

You must define the goal in complete detail. Suppose that your goal is to lose weight. That is not specific enough. What is your weight now? What would you like it to be? Your brain will not work on a goal of 'I want to lose weight.' It will work better for one of, 'I want to fit into a size 12 dress by the end of May.' Another example might be that you want a new car. What sort of car do you want – new or second-hand? What make, model, colour and extras do you want? The goal must be specific. Again I will remind you that 'what the mind of man can accurately conceive and believe it is forced to believe'.

The next stage is to set a deadline. Decide the exact date by which you want to achieve that goal. We all respond to deadlines.

Finally, bring in the real power of the untapped wealth that is your subconscious. We are just starting to learn about the incredible power of our subconscious minds. As you know, our brains never stop working, and most of the time they function without our having to give them direct instructions. You don't have to think as you walk: left foot forward, right foot forward. You just do it. But the power of our subconscious is so great that if we think about something enough, we can cause it to happen.

The body is the servant of the mind. It obeys the operations of the mind, whether they are deliberately chosen or automatically expressed. Psychologists say disease and health, like material circumstances, are rooted in thought. Sickly thoughts will express themselves in a sickly body. The people who live in fear of a disease are the people who most likely get it. Anxiety quickly demoralizes the whole body. A change of diet will not necessarily change people's thoughts. So we must all be careful what we think about, because again we have all learnt that what we think about we can bring to fruition. If we continually think we are unsuccessful, that is exactly what the outcome will be.

If we think about what we want to be or want to achieve, or vividly see ourselves owning or having something, this alone will become real, because our subconscious quite extraordinarily takes over and somehow makes it happen.

Mohammad Ali, who is acclaimed as the greatest sports personality of all time, was questioned in an interview about some of the secrets of his success. He said he was given a great body which he was determined to make the most of. Then he explained that as soon as a fight had been arranged he went into a room on his own where he could concentrate. He would then think in great depth about his tactics. The more he thought, the more he could see the conclusion, and it became so real in his mind that he could see himself winning. His picture of the end of the fight was vivid, with all of the photographers in the ring and the belt around his waist. He could actually see in his mind's eye in which round he would win the fight. You may recall that Ali used to arrange press conferences before his fights, at which he would announce in rhyming slang the round in which he would win. He was invariably right. The interviewer questioned him about visualization, and asked why, if visualization was so important, he had lost three major fights in his career. His reply was, 'On those occasions my opponent's visualization was better than mine.'

This is a big subject, and I do not intend to go into it in any depth in a book that is about the easy way to win business. But please take it on board that your most valuable asset is your brain. If you can truly visualize what you want in life, you are now really using the equipment that you have been given in a direction in which it will deliver.

I am a realist and not a theorist, and no doubt you are the same. Life does not form a continual stairway to heaven. We all have our ups and our downs, our good days and bad days, our joys and our sorrows. So if you are a realist, what about the occasions when you have a major disappointment or a crisis, or when something goes seriously wrong? Realistically life is pretty easy to cope with when everything is rosy. But to be successful or a winner in every category it is essential to be able to handle the tough times.

Let me tell you another story. When I started my working life before getting into business, I was a small farmer in Sussex. My farm covered approximately 70 acres, and I rented a further 40 acres that were some seven miles away from the home farm. One year in May I was told that my tenancy agreement on these extra acres was not to be renewed. This was the biggest crisis I had ever faced. Without that land I couldn't make the hay that was need to feed my dairy herd. I convinced myself that it would be impossible to suddenly obtain another parcel of land in the spring. I was very despondent and dreadfully worried, as I had a wife and four boys to support, and certainly no money to go out and buy land. For a few days I have to confess I wallowed in my problems, and in the process shared my worries and got the rest of the family equally worried.

I shared my dreadful situation with a friend, and he said something that has become a foundation and a philosophy for the whole of my life from that age of 26. He said, 'In every adversity there is a seed of an equivalent or greater benefit.' He went on to say, 'You must do something about this.' I did. I immediately started ringing round all of my contacts to enquire where there might be some land. I got into the car and called on people, some of whom I knew and many of whom I didn't. On the fifth day of this manic activity I found another 35 acres only a mile and a half away from my farm. The rent was a little less than I had previously been paying. We all said it turned out for the best in the end.

Now you, my reader, must have had a experience of similar gravity sometime in your life. But if you can master the downturns you have very little to ever truly fear. These days whenever I am going into a venture or new activity where there is risk involved, as well as looking on the upside I always mentally visit the downside. I want to look at the worst case scenario. Supposing it all goes wrong? What would I do to dig myself out of this hole? Having then developed a contingency plan, I no longer then think about the risk. Instead I concentrate my mind and visualize what I want to achieve.

I share this with you because it really is so successful, and I know it can work for you as it has for me and countless others.

This chapter is packed full of positive thoughts and ideas. But again as realists we must all be aware of the single most foul disease the human race has inflicted upon itself. It is said that the second most deadly instrument of destruction is the loaded gun. The first is the human tongue. The negatives that people say to each other are so foul and so evil. 'You can't do that.' 'You are no good.' 'You are a nasty person.' 'You will never achieve anything.' 'You are useless.' And equally as dangerous are the negatives that we say to ourselves. 'I am useless.' 'I can't.' 'I will never be able to.' 'I'm not lucky.' 'I'm not cut out for success.' 'I am not clever enough.'

The loaded gun may or may not be used, but the tongue destroys reputations, ruins characters, and has caused more conflict in the world than any atom bomb or weapon of destruction. The crimes committed by what people say are the causes of incredible misery throughout our planet. As a very basic example, the three Cs (criticizing, condemning and complaining) are all very harmful. Of course we all need constructive criticism, but very little criticism is constructive. No monument has ever been erected to a critic. Monuments are erected for those who have been criticized. I cannot recall any critic who will go down in history as having made a great contribution to the world.

We must all therefore be aware of this evil destroyer that holds people back from achieving so much more. Let's imagine a real-life example. You are at home in the month of September and a pretty little insect flies in through the window. It has a yellow furry body with black stripes – in short, it's a wasp. Are you likely to say to yourself, 'Oh good, a wasp has just flown in. They are such pretty creatures. I hope you'll bring your friends.' On the contrary, you will probably start immediately looking for a murder weapon – a rolled up newspaper, a fly swat or insect spray. You kill the wasp. Why? Because you know if that wasp were to land on you (which it might not) and sting you (which it also might not) it would hurt like hell. That pain would probably last for about an hour, no more. Nevertheless you will take action to stop being stung.

But if someone is negative to another person, the hurt doesn't last for an hour. It could last for days, weeks, months, years and sometimes a lifetime. A person's direction, belief and confidence can be destroyed by what someone else says. So protect your most valuable asset, and equally as important, do not put your mind into self-destruct mode by indulging in negative thoughts about yourself or other people.

The negative thoughts we have about others are equally as damaging as any negative thoughts we have about ourselves. Those thoughts can turn to hatred, which can become a killer. We can make ourselves ill or even do harm to another person.

This is all in your control. You can change a nasty thought instantly by just saying to yourself, 'I am not going to think that.' Replace it with a positive thought. Just take it for granted that you were born with a positive brain, and it is your responsibility to keep it that way.

Pocket Reminders

■ Don't catch affluenza.
■ Oxygenate the brain.
■ Set your goals.
■ Use your subconscious mind.
■ Visualize what you really want.
■ In every adversity there is the seed of an equivalent or greater benefit.
■ Avoid the negatives.

Wise words

Yesterday is history. Tomorrow is a mystery. Today is a gift. That is why it is called the present.

13

How to Fail Fast

This short chapter is for those who really do not want to be a business winner, and have probably been told to read this book by their boss. It is also for others who have a lemming-like approach to failure.

If that is you, why spend years in attempting to fail? Do it fast.

Easy steps

- It's not your responsibility to win business. Anyhow, good products and services sell themselves. You didn't spend years of qualifying to become a sales person, so stick to your profession and don't get caught up with all this nonsense about winning business.
- Develop a frame of mind that your life would be so much easier and stressful without clients or customers. They are just a pain in the neck.
- Whatever you do, don't plan your days. Under no circumstances make a 'to do' list. Always make sure that each day you do the things you enjoy doing, and put off the nasty jobs.

■ If by some misfortune you get an enquiry for business it is not necessary to respond to it quickly, as you have much more important tasks. If you don't respond quickly, with a little bit of luck the enquirer will go to a competitor.

■ If you are asked to return a phone call – don't. Let the person phone again. Remember you are busy. You have more important things to do than speak to clients or customers.

■ Whatever you do, do not be proactive about getting new business. This is crucial as you know proactivity wins new business.

■ If your boss is going to make your life hell by insisting that you bring in new business, tell him or her that what you need is a sales course that teaches closing techniques, and that the secret of good selling is to make people buy things they don't want or need.

■ You really should be embarrassed about your fees and prices. If you aren't, then get embarrassed. Offer hefty discounts as it really is so important to be the cheapest in today's world.

■ Under no circumstances give a money-back guarantee. All clients and customers are crooks and they will try to rip you off.

■ Pride yourself in your service, and don't worry about improving on it. It doesn't matter a damn what the customers think. Anyhow, why should you worry about all of this customer care nonsense? People are very lucky to have your services and products.

■ If by some terrible mishap you are required to give a proposal or quote, there is no rush. Only do it when you have done much more important tasks. When you eventually mail it, finish your covering letter by saying, 'If I can be of any further service please don't hesitate to contact me.'

■ The next move is always the customer's or client's responsibility.

▦ It's your life so you wear anything you like that makes you feel comfortable. Other people should accept you for what you are. If they have difficulties with that, well, that's their problem.

▦ If you are dragged into some awful (because it's beneath you) selling situation, it is your duty to make sure that the prospect knows how brilliant you are. Tell him or her your life story, and how useless everybody else is in your firm. Don't forget to tell the person about your hobbies and interests, and best of all show some pictures of your last holiday.

▦ Please don't waste any of your valuable time by showing interest in anyone else's problems or worries, particularly clients or potential clients or customers.

▦ If you are in business for yourself, spend all your available money on advertising, then you can go broke gradually, waiting for the phone to ring.

▦ If you do decide to put out an advertisement, it must have lots of copy but no visuals, and should be all about your company and its products and services. Definitely do not include anything that shows results that people might like or want.

▦ Hopefully you won't be getting any new customers and with a little bit of luck your existing customers are going elsewhere. This will make your life so much easier. Fortunately the money will be running out so now is the time to get really aggressive and finish your business off.

▦ Really, you must develop a reputation for being unreliable. It will seriously annoy any customers or clients you have.

▦ Put off until tomorrow what you can do today.

▦ You don't need any pocket reminders because you will doing these things anyhow, hopefully.

Wise words

Show your contempt for the person and your concern for the problem – that is, if you are really bent on failure.

Tablets of stone

- ▦ Be interested to be interesting.

- ▦ Ask the right questions to get the right answers.

- ▦ Always *take* proposals.

- ▦ Have a database of prospects.

- ▦ Value your 'to do' list.

- ▦ Identify your customer profile.

- ▦ Step into other people's shoes.

- ▦ Make a daily 'to do' list.

- ▦ Never give the next move to a prospect.

- ▦ Explain the results of your product or service first.

- ▦ Genuinely care for your customers/clients.

- ▦ Practise risk reversal.

- ▦ Send one caring note a week.

- ▦ Value the 'no, not today' list.

- ▦ Be proud of your prices or fees.

Failure isn't fatal

Failure isn't fatal,
Though it seems so at the time.

Failure can be hurtful
When desire to win isn't prime.

Failure's face is ugly
Like the Dame in pantomime.

Failure is the chance you
Take when mountains you will climb.

Failure isn't fatal,
Try again and win next time.

Failure is not illegal,
Never trying is the crime!

Freddie Mitman

References

Carnegie, Dale (1953) *How to Win Friends and Influence People*, Cedar Books/Hutchinson, London

Denny, Richard (2006) *Succeed for Yourself: Unlock your potential for success and happiness*, rev edn, Kogan Page, London

Denny, Richard (2006) *Selling to Win*, 3rd edn, Kogan Page, London

Goleman, Daniel (1996) *Emotional Intelligence*, Bloomsbury, London

Mellor, Laurie (2003) *Sales Success in Tough Times*, Dream Depot, Littlehampton

Peters, Thomas J and Waterman, Robert H (2004) *In Search of Excellence*, rev edn, Profile, London

Pegg, Mike (1994) *Positive Leadership: How to Build a Winning Team*, Management Books 2000, Cirencester

ALSO AVAILABLE FROM KOGAN PAGE

ALSO AVAILABLE FROM KOGAN PAGE

Each page is packed with easy to read common-sense advice on how to turn dreams into goals and goals into success."

Roger Black

"Richard Denny is the master of motivation. If you read this book it will probably change your life."

Rosemary Conley

ISBN: 978 0 7494 4436 5   Paperback   2006

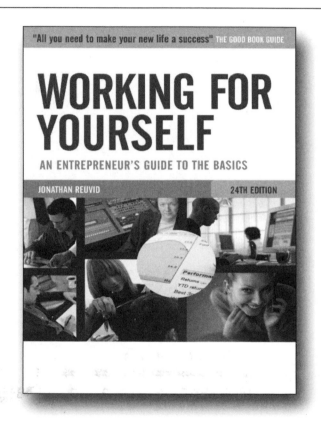